RELIGIONS OF ANCIENT INDIA

RELIGIONS OF ANCIENT INDIA

LOUIS RENOU

SCHOCKEN BOOKS · NEW YORK

First SCHOCKEN edition 1968

This edition published by arrangement with The Athlone Press
Library of Congress Catalog Card No. 68-16660

Manufactured in the United States of America

THE LOUIS H. JORDAN BEQUEST

The will of the Rev. Louis H. Jordan provided that the greater part of his estate should be paid over to the School of Oriental and African Studies to be employed for the furtherance of studies in comparative religion to which his life had been devoted. Part of the funds which thus became available was to be used for the endowment of a Louis H. Jordan Lectureship in Comparative Religion. The lecturer, appointed annually, is required to deliver a course of six or eight lectures on comparative religion, for subsequent publication. The first series of lectures was delivered in 1951.

PREFACE

THESE lectures were delivered (in a slightly abridged form) in May 1951, at the School of Oriental and African Studies of the University of London, when I had the honour of being invited by the Director and the Academic Board of the School to give the first series of six lectures under the Louis H. Jordan Bequest, on the Religions of India.

The field surveyed in the summary studies that follow is so vast—with the exception of Buddhism, it embraces all the religious manifestations of India, past and present—that inevitably many aspects are only briefly treated, while others receive no more than a cursory mention. The reader desirous of more detailed information will find references in the footnotes to the bibliography of the principal questions dealt with.

My intention in these lectures was to give an account of the present state of the main problems. The detailed scholarly studies which constitute the standard works on the subject, and which provide the basis and justification of all contemporary work, do not always enable the reader to see the facts with which they deal in their proper perspective and in their relationship to the general background. It is useful to take stock of our position from time to time, so that we can form some estimate of the stage that our researches have reached, whether they have made progress, or whether the position is merely stationary or even perhaps less assured than it seemed before. The world of Indology is constantly evolving; and while fresh views are continually being advocated, the research work that is an essential preliminary to new advances, editions of texts, studies of vocabulary, learned monographs and so on, follows more slowly and usually avoids the conclusions that more impatient theorists wish to see adopted at all costs. In this study I have tried to advance moderate, and, as I hope, reasonable views.

There remains the pleasant duty of expressing my thanks to Miss Sheila M. Fynn, Assistant Lecturer at the School of Oriental and African Studies, for her clear and accurate English translation of a text which, I am afraid, was not particularly easy.

L. R.

CONTENTS

RELIGIONS OF ANCIENT INDIA

I

Vedism: I

There was a time, not very long ago, when every Indianist (especially those of the German school) considered that a monograph on Vedism, or an edition of a Vedic text, was an ideal first piece of research to undertake. The fact that Vedic studies no longer occupy such a focal position is probably the outcome of this earlier concentration on them to the relative neglect of other fields. The student is likely to feel that there is nothing left to discover (although in this he would be wrong), or at least that what remains to be discovered would not repay the time and trouble needed to attain a mastery of the subject.

Another reason for this decline of interest is the isolation of the Veda. Nowadays our attention is centred on cultural influences and points of contact between civilizations. The Veda provides little of this sort of material, for it developed in seclusion. Yet perhaps it is really more important to begin by studying individual manifestations in and for themselves, and to examine their own internal structure.

In this field of research we have an exceptionally good collection of works of reference; there is no lack of dictionaries, grammars, editions, translations and monographs on various aspects of the religion. Though much remains still to be done, the work already accomplished has been carried out with greater thoroughness than is the case in many other branches of Indian studies. Yet we cannot say that a satisfactory picture of the subject as a whole has been achieved, and a sense of frustration pervades the present state of Vedic studies. The healthy scepticism of Whitney and, more recently, of Keith, may have contributed to the present uncertainty, no less than the over-enthusiasm of various other research workers, both in Europe and in India.

In the first place, no definite chronology can be established, and this is an embarrassment to Western scholars. The position is admittedly the same in many other fields of Indian studies, for example in that of early Buddhism: but in that case there is at least a basis for discussion. It is clear that the oldest Vedic texts in their earliest redactions are posterior to the Aryan invasion of India. But this gives us only a very rough indication of date, especially in the case of *mantras* where it is essential to distinguish between the gradual process of the composition of texts, and their 'oral transcription' as we know it today. This transcription developed late, under the impetus of a rapidly changing language. The *mantras*, even those of the *Ṛgveda*, represent a fairly late stage of phonetic development: their language is not entirely homogeneous, and moreover diverges appreciably from the forms which we can occasionally restore on the evidence of the metre. We often hear it stated that the textual tradition of the Veda has been handed down with scrupulous exactitude; but this statement needs qualification. From the time when it was established in its traditional form, the *Ṛgveda* has in fact been carefully preserved from any alteration. We know this from present-day recitations, which correspond exactly to the rules given in the *Prātiśākhyas*. But before this, throughout the long centuries during which the hymns were composed and handed down within individual families, and used at ceremonies, they were exposed to change. The literary forms of the other texts were established on widely varying principles. Many treatises have been lost or damaged, entire schools have fallen into oblivion; side by side with a rigorous conservatism such as that of the *Śatapatha-Brāhmaṇa*, we find a corrupt text like the *Paippalāda* recension of the *Atharvaveda*. One has only to consult the *Vedic Variants*[1] to realize that the changelessness of the Veda is a fiction.

In the late nineteenth century various erroneous speculations on the chronology of the Veda were advanced, and these did great disservice to the subject. It is regrettable that a scholar of Hermann Jacobi's eminence should have been associated with such misconceptions.[2]

It was at first hoped that the discoveries at Harappa and Mohenjo-Daro might throw some light on the Veda; but this hope was not fulfilled. What is known as the Indus civilization appears to owe nothing to the Veda, for indeed, in its origins at least, it is definitely of earlier date; nor does it appear that the Veda owes anything to it. The Aryan tribes may well have overrun it without in any way being influenced by it, settling on the ruins of a decayed or decaying empire. If the forms of religion revealed in the seals and figurines of the Indus have any remote connection with Indian forms, it is not so much with those of Vedism as with those of Hinduism, a Hinduism which, though known to us only by inference, must have already existed in Vedic times, and probably considerably earlier. The Harappa inscriptions would no doubt tell us more on this subject, but until they are deciphered it is idle to try to explain the war of the Ten Kings as a clash between the people of the Indus

[1] An unfinished work, begun by M. Bloomfield and F. Edgerton, continued by M. B. Emeneau. Three volumes have appeared so far (Philadelphia, 1930–34): i, *The Verb*; ii, *Phonetics*; iii, *Noun and Pronoun Inflection*.

[2] Cf. 'Über das Alter des Ṛgveda', *Festgruss R. Roth* (1893), p. 68; 'Beiträge zur Kenntniss der Vedischen Chronologie', *Götting. Nachr.* (1894), p. 105; 'Der Vedische Kalender und das Alter des Veda', *Z. dtsch. morgenländ. Ges.*, 49, p. 218; 'Nochmals über das Alter des Veda', *ibid.*, 50, p. 69. *Contra* (among others) A. Barth, *J. Asiat.*, 1894, 1st part, p. 156 (= *Works* of Barth, iv, p. 168); H. Oldenberg, *Z. dtsch. morgenländ Ges.*, 48, p. 629; 49, p. 470; 50, p. 423.

and the Aryan invaders, or to connect the name 'Harappa' with the river or region called Hariyūpīyā. In the very primitive architecture which we can infer from descriptions in the Vedic ritual texts there is nothing that can reasonably be compared with the buildings of Mohenjo-Daro, unless we postulate a social and artistic retrogression incompatible with the high spiritual plane of the hymns. In short, we are faced with complete defeat in this quarter.

It seemed possible at one time that a guiding date had been found in an Anatolian text mentioning a treaty between a Hittite king and a prince of Mitanni, which attested the existence of certain divine names in the fourteenth century B.C. But this unexpected explicitness as to date only opened up new problems: does the text really refer to Vedic gods, or does it refer to Indo-Iranian gods? Had they been brought from India by emigrants or colonists, or were they at this date only moving towards India? At the most, the treaty of Mitanni attests the existence in the fourteenth century of a series of divine names of the Vedic type; it gives no evidence of established texts or fixed forms of religion at this time.

The geographical environment of the Veda is equally uncertain. We have, of course, an approximate indication of where the Vedic tribes were situated; it is possible to pick out Iranian features, or rather, features of modern Afghanistan, from a background of a more specifically Indian type. This limited horizon gradually widens towards the east to reach the Ganges, and certain scholars take it for granted that a late text like the *Śatapatha-Brāhmaṇa* can be located in Videha, the modern Bihar, on the borders of Bengal. This is too bold a supposition. All the Vedic texts, including the *Śatapatha*, originate either in the Upper Indus or in the region known as the Kurupañcālas which forms the natural eastward continuation of the plains of the Punjab. Admittedly, tradition has it that there were schools, and therefore texts, in central and southern India, and mediaeval inscriptions confirm this dispersal. But the establishment of these schools was much later than the composition of the texts. It is important to remember that the source of Vedic inspiration is a single fountain-head, from which many streams flowed out in course of time. We are constantly brought back to this idea of a Veda existing before the schools, incorporating in itself a mythology and an agreed ritual, that had arisen in the original Vedic community of clans and families. We cannot explain the literary diversity of Vedism except by postulating an original unity, and it is unfortunate that this 'Ur-Veda' cannot be reconstructed with any certainty from the texts in our possession. The scholar is confronted by similar situations in many other branches of Indology.

We are hardly in a better position to describe the decline of Vedism. We know that the official cult lapsed (to be revived later, more or less artificially); the private cult underwent transformations; the mythology, which was probably becoming archaic at the time of the *Ṛgveda*, was reconstituted. But there is no means of assigning a time or place to these changes. We are reduced in the end to a purely formal definition of Vedism: any text composed in a certain style and following a certain pattern is Vedic. It must, of course, be understood that creative literary activity in this field eventually gives place to the endless elaboration of commentaries.

The texts are in fact our only means of defining this religion, which has left us no archaeological evidence, and which possesses no dogma or founder, no church or history. In spite of the profound imprint it has left on later Indian culture, Vedism in its formative period had no far-reaching influence. The Vedic clans, or *Āryas*, as they called themselves, were surrounded by the hostile mass of indigenous *dāsas*, a dark-skinned pre-Aryan people who may have been

Dravidians. The clans themselves were divided: there were the *aris* or 'strangers' who were sometimes allies or protectors, but more often rivals to be watched. There were the *vrātyas*, whose religion Vedism tried to absorb into itself, and whose texts may have been incorporated into the *Atharvaveda*.

It is idle to look for a historical pattern underlying this terminology: but none the less it is possible to see in the descriptions of battles, alliances and quarrels, especially those of the Indra cycle, a gradual transformation of chieftains and tribes into demi-gods, demons and divine cohorts. The very ambiguity of this mythology reflects the vicissitudes of a community living in constant danger.

Vedism was in the charge of a priestly élite who served a military aristocracy; it may well be that the masses were already Hindu. The private or domestic cult was only Hindu practice with a veneer of hieratic formulae. The ceremonial cult represented true Vedism, together with the orthodox mythological traditions, the solemn religious festivals and the poetic and other contests which were included in them. It was, however, by no means a public cult.

If we look once again at the chronological side of the subject, we shall see that the end of what is usually called the Vedic period does not coincide with the beginning of literary Hinduism nor with the beginning of the Buddhist and Jaina movements. The links between Vedism and the great epics, the earliest non-Vedic texts that we possess, are extremely slender. The Kurus and their King Parikṣit, before whose son the *Mahābhārata* was first recited, are mentioned as almost legendary figures in the *Bṛhadāraṇyaka-Upaniṣad*. According to the statements of the *Purāṇas* (which must be treated cautiously), the war described in the *Mahābhārata* took place at a date corresponding to 1400 B.C.: this would then be the time of Parikṣit, who is spoken of as a living ruler in the *Atharvaveda*. It has also been pointed out that another *Upaniṣad*, the *Chāndogya*, mentions the name of Kṛṣṇa Devakīputra as a Brahman student, and that this is evidently a reference to the hero who was an ally of the Pāṇḍavas. The links with the *Rāmāyaṇa* are of the same type, though even less conclusive: King Janaka of Videha, father of the Princess Sītā, is an important figure in the latter part of the *Śatapatha*. There is nothing in all this on which a relative chronology could be based: but one can sense a 'sentimental' connection between the last stirrings of the old theocracy and the secular society which was to produce the Epic.

The connections with Buddhism are very deceptive. Ever since Kern,[1] of course, analogies have been seen between Vedism and the *Hīnayāna*, and more particularly between the domestic *sūtras* and the *Prātimokṣa*; but the explanation lies not in borrowing but in a basis of thought common to both. The danger in considering Indian religions as separate groups of phenomena is that one tends to forget that certain essentially Indian features characterize them all. Other scholars, venturing into the realms of speculation, have pointed out resemblances between the Vedic mysteries centring on the fire-altar, and certain features of the Buddhist cosmology which might be described as architectural mysticism. Senart[2] drew attention to various episodes in the life of the Buddha which could be interpreted in accordance with the old myths. These comparisons can be multiplied indefinitely, but we must not read too much into them. The *Upaniṣads* are a particularly delicate case; the problem, stated in simplified form, has been whether the *Upaniṣads* were pre- or post-Buddhist. Their subject-matter and method of presentation

[1] Cf. J. C. H. Kern, *Geschiedenis van het Buddhism in Indie* (Harlem, 1881; French translation, Paris, 1901); and *Manual of Indian Buddhism* (Strassburg, 1896).

[2] Émile Senart, *Essai sur la légende du Buddha, son caractère et ses origines* (Paris, 1875; 2nd edition, 1882).

have much in common with Buddhistic writings; the Pāli style seems, indeed, to be a diluted imitation of the Upaniṣadic style. The secular approach of the *Upaniṣads* is characteristic also of Buddhism and Jainism, those religions of princes. If we work on the presupposition that in India progress is from the simple to the complex, from brevity to elaboration, then the *Upaniṣads* must be regarded as earlier. This is my own view. But we must not be surprised to see that in India parallel streams of thought may exist side by side without any contact other than an unemphatic rivalry. If, on the other hand, we believe that the *Upaniṣads* were only made possible through Buddhist influence, or, in other words, that 'it was Buddhism that taught the Indians to philosophize', we are losing sight of the fact that Vedic speculation is firmly established from the *Ṛgveda* onwards, not only in the tenth book, which summarizes a great mass of speculative material, but even in what is known as the older *Ṛgveda*, for example, in iii. 54, 9: 'I recognize from afar the ancient and immemorial one. We are descended from him, the great Procreator, the Father. The gods who do him homage, in their own vast, separate domain, quickly took up their positions in the intervening space . . .' Here we already have a full formulation: the single original principle, and the realm of the gods lying between Man and the Supreme Being. Religion and speculation go hand in hand from the very outset.

If we cannot establish an absolute chronology, let us see where there is any hope of setting up an internal relative one. According to Max Müller,[1] the Vedic age extends over four great periods, each one lasting for centuries. In the first period the hymns were composed, in the second they were established in set forms, in the third commentaries were composed on them, and in the final period the

[1] Cf. esp. *A History of Ancient Sanskrit Literature* (London, 1859; later editions, 1860 etc.).

rites with which they are connected were described. In the same way others have postulated an epic age, and a canonical Jaina or Buddhist period. To cover any stretches of time not thus accounted for, the decline and subsequent renaissance of Hindu civilization has been invoked.

It is always dangerous to base a chronology on literature. It is clear that the Vedic hymns as a whole date back to a period before the commentaries and descriptions; but they are not evidence of a spontaneous aesthetic response to natural phenomena. They presuppose an established religion of which our knowledge is imperfect, but which must have borne some resemblance to that described in the later *Kalpa*. Only in the *Yajur-Veda* do we get a full idea of it; and in the *yajus* the so-called *mantra* and *brāhmaṇa* periods are indistinguishable, according to Max Müller. Some scholars have maintained that certain parts of the *Vājasaneyi-Saṃhitā* were composed after the *Śatapatha*; and Caland held that the *sūtras* cannot be assigned to any specific period.[1] We are led to the conclusion that some texts attained their definitive form at an older period of the language than others. Sylvain Lévi held the paradoxical theory that there was no Vedic chronological problem and that all the Vedic works were compiled together at one and the same time, relatively late.[2] Similarly, Darmesteter considered the *gāthās* to be a late text, which differed from the bulk of the *Avesta* in orthography only.[3] There is some truth underlying these theories: the establishment of the texts from a combination of scattered sources must have

[1] W. Caland in *Götting. gelehr. Anz.*, 1902, p. 122; edition of the *Śatapatha-Brāhmaṇa in the Kāṇvīya Recension*, i, 99.

[2] This theory was put forward in his lectures, and is remembered by those who attended them (cf. L. Renou, 'Sylvain Lévi et son œuvre scientifique', *J. Asiat.*, 1936, 1st part, p. 17); v. *Mémorial Sylvain Lévi* (Paris, 1938), p. 8, and *L'Inde Civilisatrice* (Paris, 1938), p. 35.

[3] Cf. esp. the introduction to his English translation of the *Zend-Avesta* in the *Sacred Books of the East* (French translation, Paris, 1892–93).

taken place at one definite period, in response to a common demand; but the material used dated from widely differing periods of antiquity.

The *Ṛgveda* is much more than an adjunct to ritual. It might be called a literary anthology, drawn from family traditions. The religious expressions found in it are poetic exordia to the cult, and are not designed as the direct accompaniment of ceremonies. We see something of the same kind in the *Prātaranuvāka* of the *Agniṣṭoma*. I imagine that the works which have survived are those which fulfilled the requirements of a poetic competition. It has been pointed out that the hymns suggest the atmosphere of a contest in eloquence. The aim was to compose on a given theme, or perhaps according to a given plan, not introducing direct accounts of the lives of the gods so much as veiled allusions, occult correspondences between the sacred and the profane, such as still form the foundation of Indian speculative thought. A large part of Sanskrit literature is esoteric. These correspondences, and the magic power they emanate, are called *brahman*: this is the oldest sense of the term. They are not intellectual conceptions but experiences which have been lived through at the culmination of a state of mystic exaltation conceived as revelation. The *soma* is the catalyst of these latent forces. The designation *kavi* is given to the poet who can seize and express these correspondences, and to the god who sends him inspiration. The term *vipra*, literally 'the quivering one', is also used. This suggests the mystical quivering described by the Kashmiri *Spanda* school. Traces of this mystical intoxication can often be found in cult practice. The *kavi* of the classical period, the learned poet, transposes the old Vedic ambiguity to the aesthetic plane by means of double meanings and multiple senses; the classical *vakrokti*, 'tortuous speech', calls to mind the epithet *vaṅkuḥ kaviḥ* used of Rudra. This is the reason for the intricacies of Vedic style and vocabulary. A contributory factor, too, was the Indo-Iranian tradition of verbal esotericism, evidenced by the *gāthās*. Moreover, *śaṃsa* (praise) is sacred in itself: the man who has the gift of *śaṃsa* receives it from a god in the same manner as a material gift.

But on the whole the *raison d'être* of the hymns lies in the cult. Bergaigne showed that many of them were composed with a definite liturgical purpose in view.[1] He may have pursued this line of thought a little too far, but it is a pity that his researches, like those of so many others, were interrupted. Some hymns were undoubtedly only accessory to the liturgy, some were entirely secular in tone; others may show a reaction against liturgical dominance. They were all pressed into use by those who compiled the final ritual forms, just as the Avestic *gāthās* were used in a sacrifice for which they were not originally intended.

We cannot, however, reconstruct this early cult. Our sole data would be the *soma* ceremonies, which are the only rituals that the hymns treat in detail. In these rites alone does the *hotṛ* play a part, and the *Ṛgveda* is primarily the manual of the *hotṛ* and of the *udgātṛ* (for whom a special text, the *Sāmaveda*, was later compiled). But the *Ṛgveda*, although it describes the preparation of the *soma* at great length, hardly mentions the other operations which, together with the *soma*, make up the ritual of the great sacrifices. Animal sacrifices, for example, are barely touched upon. In order to understand the nature of the early Vedic cult we should need to possess the formulary of the *adhvaryu*, the officiating priest. In the *Yajurveda* we have a much later version of this, in the recensions of several distinct schools, and full of borrowings from the *Ṛgveda*. We should also need the *paddhati*, a guide which would enable us to follow a ceremony contemporary with the hymns.

[1] A. Bergaigne, 'Recherches sur l'histoire de la liturgie védique', *J. Asiat.*, 1889, 1st part, pp. 5 and 121.

At first sight it seems that we are better informed on the subject of Vedic mythology. There are few hymns which do not contain mythical allusions of some kind, and many of them abound with references to the exploits and adventures of the gods. But it is impossible to establish a history of the gods from this material, obscured as it is by the constant repetition of the same phrases in different contexts. We are really dealing not so much with individual gods as with mythological contexts, founded on what Max Müller called 'henotheism'.[1] The term was later ridiculed; but it expressed his meaning, and represents a permanent feature of Indian thought, which is especially noticeable in Śāktism. It is the tendency of the worshipper to ascribe the attributes of other gods to the particular deity whom he is honouring. The mythology of the *Ṛgveda* is confused, with no beginning or end; it is a mythology in the making, constantly relating itself to the process of the Creation, and to the theme of the early ages of the world.

We can, of course, invoke external evidence to throw light on these allusions. The history of religion gives us some guidance in classifying mythological types, and the evidence of later India must not be overlooked. In the last twenty years there has in fact been a rehabilitation in the methods of comparative mythology, due to M. Dumézil.[2] The reforms of Zoroaster obscure the surviving Indo-

[1] In many of his works, and especially in the *Lectures on the Origin and Growth of Religion, as illustrated by the Religions of India* (London, 1878; later editions, 1882 etc.).

[2] Cf. his early works *Le Festin d'Immortalité* (Paris, 1924); *Le Problème des Centaures* (Paris, 1929). Others dealing more specifically with Vedic material are: *Ouranos-Varuṇa* (Paris, 1934); *Mitra-Varuṇa*, 1940; 2nd edition, 1948; *Jupiter, Mars, Quirinus, Essai sur la conception indo-européenne de la société et sur les origines de Rome*, 1941; *Naissance de Rome* (=*Jupiter, Mars, Quirinus*, II), 1944; *Naissance d'archanges* (=*Jupiter Mars, Quirinus*, III), 1945; *Jupiter, Mars, Quirinus*, IV, *Explications de textes indiens et latins*, 1948; *Servius et la Fortune, Essai sur la fonction sociale de louange et de blâme* (etc.), 1943; *Tarpeia, Cinq essais de philologie comparative*, 1947; *Le Troisième Souverain*, 1949.

Iranian features, but traces of them can be perceived in the recent *Avesta*, especially in the *Yašts*, which have not been fully explored from this point of view. The blurred outline of a resemblance can be traced between Ahura Mazdāh and the Vedic Varuṇa. The Aməša Spəntas, formerly thought to be connected with the Ādityas, now seem more likely to be a transposition to the abstract plane of a series beginning with Varuṇa and Mitra, and continuing through Indra to the Aśvins and others.[1]

Vedic mythology, like most Indian mythologies, contains material which it is tempting to label as non-Aryan or pre-Aryan, though no precise meaning can be attached to these terms. M. Kuiper recently discerned a 'proto-Munda' myth, as he called it, in the Veda: the story of an archer-god who kills the boar Emuṣa with his bow *drumbhūlī*.[2] The fact remains that the representations of the Divine in the Veda form an impressive and unified whole, even though occasional elements are borrowed, just as a great writer uses words from many sources. The synthesis is a new systemic creation which owes little to what it has inherited or borrowed.

Various planes are discernible in this mythology. On the farthest plane, practically without mythology, are Dyaus Pitar and Pṛthivī (Heaven and Earth). In the middle distance is the figure of Varuṇa, already fallen in some of the hymns. With him we associate the age without *ṛta*, the state of primeval anarchy which he brought to an end. In the foreground stand Indra and his great cycle, aggressive gods, who have absorbed the substance of many other figures into themselves and now dominate mythical legend, have the monopoly of relationships with the human race,

[1] Cf. Dumézil, *Naissance d'archanges*, p. 56.

[2] 'An Austro-Asiatic Myth in the Rigveda', *Mededeelingen d. koninkl. Nederl. Akad. van Wetenschappen*, Afd. Letterk., Nieuwe Reeks, Deel 13 (1950), no. 7.

and are the chief protagonists in struggles against the demons. Viṣṇu and Rudra seem to be relatively new figures. These various groups are linked together by the agency of beings such as the Maruts and the Rudras. Lastly the Fire in all its forms, the sacrificial Plant and the *soma*, the liquor distilled from it, were given divine status and incorporated into the legend of one of the gods; Bergaigne[1] has clearly shown that the entire Vedic mythology was reshaped or at any rate reorientated as a setting for Agni and Soma, and that all the other divinities became counterparts or reflections of them.

The subject is still further complicated by the fact that in the doings of the gods there are several levels of significance. In part they are the transposition of natural phenomena to the mythical plane. Vedic nature-worship, though it was over-emphasized by Max Müller[2] and perhaps also by Macdonell[3] and Keith,[4] is undeniable. We cannot, of course, admit that lunar myth is as omnipresent as Hillebrandt maintained,[5] nor can we consent fully to Oldenberg's thesis of planetary representations.[6] But at all events the Sun is an all-pervading, ever-present force, shown in many forms, now directly, now symbolically. If it is true that the *ṛṣis* did all they could to obscure the lines of approach that would have indicated a 'naturalist' interpretation, it would account for much of the occultism of the Veda, or the Vedic '*galimatias*', as it used to be called.

[1] *La religion védique d'après les Hymnes du Rig-Veda* (3 vols., Paris, 1878); cf. especially vol. i, p. xiii.

[2] Op. cit.; also elsewhere, e.g. in *Natural Religion* (London, 1888; later editions, 1892 etc.).

[3] A. A. Macdonell, *Vedic Mythology* (Strassburg, 1897), *passim*.

[4] A. B. Keith, *The Religion and Philosophy of the Veda and Upanishads* (Cambridge, Mass., 1925), esp. p. 58.

[5] A. Hillebrandt, *Vedische Mythologie* (3 vols., Breslau, 1891–1902; 2nd edition, 2 vols., 1927–29).

[6] H. Oldenberg, *Die Religion des Veda* (Berlin, 1894; 3rd edition, 1923); 'Varuṇa und die Ādityas', *Z. dtsch. morgenländ. Ges.*, 50, p. 43.

M. Wikander[1] was led by ethnographical analogies to suppose that the Maruts represented a group of young men formed with an initiation ceremony in view. But this only amounts to saying that we must at all costs discover in the Veda an institution that exists in other more or less primitive cultures. M. Goossens recently produced an ingenious theory: starting from the hypothesis of M. Grégoire, that Asklepios, the son of Apollo, was originally the god of mole-hills and the founder of a mole-cult, he then draws attention to a certain formula of the *Yajus* in which the mole is called Rudra's animal. On this basis he builds up an ambitious mythological edifice with the object of identifying Apollo and Rudra.[2] But in this case there is not even the phonetic similarity which gives some support to the identification of Ouranos with Varuṇa, for example. The great multivalency and indefiniteness of Vedic legend suggest all kinds of associations to the mind which when formulated prove insubstantial.

M. Dumézil has made a valuable contribution in bringing to light the various social functions which underlie Indo-European mythology; these functions are respectively religious and juridical, military and temporal, and economic.[3] M. Benveniste in fact found traces of a tripartite social system in the Veda,[4] and it is possible that certain aspects of the representations of the divine and of the ritual itself reflect a threefold arrangement. But tripartition takes many forms in the Veda, and there is nothing to indicate that it is an image of a social framework which is hardly even mentioned in the Vedic hymns. In any case

[1] Stig Wikander, *Der arische Männerbund* (Lund, 1938).

[2] H. Grégoire in collaboration with R. Goossens and M. Mathieu, *Asklépios, Apollon Smintheus et Rudra* (Brussels, 1950).

[3] Cf. works cited above, p. 12, n. 2, and chapter 1 of *The Indo-European Heritage in Rome* (London, 1949).

[4] Émile Benveniste, 'Traditions indo-iraniennes sur les classes sociales', *J. Asiat.*, 1938, 2nd part, p. 529.

this explanation would cover only a very small proportion of the total instances in the Veda.

There are many factors which might lead us to interpret mythology in terms of ritual. Such interpretations have been attempted for the *Sautrāmaṇī* and the *Pravargya*, for example. But here again the difficulties are formidable. It is often possible to discern certain correspondences between a particular formula and its accompanying rite, but we cannot be sure whether we are dealing with an authentic original parallelism or with a later adaptation, made perhaps by playing on the words. In magical prayers the correspondences are striking; they are remarkable too in domestic rites, but in the official ceremonial they occur more rarely. The most important mythical episodes, those which reflect cosmogonic events, have no ritual equivalencies; and in general they are not used in any way in the classical ceremonies. We must be content with very general theories if we are to avoid arbitrary explanations such as those put forward in the old *Brāhmaṇas*, where we find fabricated accounts of the origin of various details in the liturgical ceremonial. In these stories there is much that deserves attention, but the *nidāna* or *bandhu*, the hidden connection that they try to establish, cannot be accepted; it is too visibly the product of the priestly mind. It is recognized in the texts that comprehension must cease at a certain point: they declare '*paro'kṣakāmā hi devāḥ*', 'the gods love what is cryptic'.

The complexity of Vedic material is already recognized in the *Nirukta*, which takes account of several methods of exegesis. In company with the theories already surveyed, especially the suggestion, difficult of proof, that historical events were transmuted into myth, we must consider the part played by 'ethnological' explanations: these are often clearly justified, but if too much emphasis is laid on them the individuality of particular variations tends to become absorbed into the undifferentiated substratum. We may reject the psychical explanation, which occasionally appears in native exegesis, and which Aurobindo tried to revive.[1] According to this theory the Veda is a vast piece of symbolism representing the passions of the soul and its striving after higher spiritual planes: thus the Veda, we are told, ceases to be a barbarous and unintelligible hymnary. I fear that it also ceases to be a document of prehistory and becomes a manual of modern theosophy. Such an obvious anachronism is not likely to convince any serious student.

If we had to choose one theory to work on, out of so many passed in review and seen to be untenable, the preference would go to that of Bergaigne. His work, neglected in his lifetime, has steadily gained in stature. We could not adopt unaltered his general theory of interpretation, according to which all mythological portrayals are variants of the sacred fire and the sacrificial liquor. But he has shown us the right method, the method of seeking correspondences between the world of men, the performers of the sacrifice, the microcosm on the one hand, and the 'aerial' world of the gods, the macrocosm, on the other. The duty of the *ṛṣis* was to ensure the ordered functioning of the world and of religious ceremonial by reproducing the succession of cosmic events, the *ordo rerum*, in their acts and in the imagery they conceived. The term *ṛta* is a designation of the cosmic order on which human order, ethics and social behaviour depend. Analogous terms such as *dharman*, *dhāman*, *kratu* and many others have a twofold application according to whether they refer to man or the gods, *adhyātmam* or *adhidaivatam*, as the *Upaniṣads* say. Seen in this light, the Veda is a vast magical synthesis expressed in symbolic terms. The images of the Veda have a ritual significance in themselves; they bring about the ordered functioning of a universe which is itself conceived as the scene

[1] Cf. *Hymns to the Mystic Fire* (Pondicherry, 1946), p. xlviii.

of a vast sacrifice, the prototype of man-made sacrifices. Thus Vedism is already *Yoga*, a collective *Yoga* in which the composers of formulae, the early ancestors who inaugurated the sacrifice, and the gods who are both witnesses and participants, all play their part.

This, then, is the origin of Vedic esotericism, which, as we have seen, is linked with the esotericism of later India, as it appears in the *Tantras*, in learned poetry, in the theories of aesthetics on which this poetry is based, and even in legal tradition. The Indian mind is constantly seeking hidden correspondences between things which belong to entirely distinct conceptual systems.

In the *Upaniṣads*, all these correspondences are reduced to the comprehensive equation *ātman/brahman*, which appeared to the new *kavis* as a *résumé* of the whole of Vedic thought. The word *upaniṣad* itself, as it is first used in the *Śatapatha Brāhmaṇa*, means only 'equivalence'. According to *Ś.B.* X. 4, 5, 1, the function of the *upaniṣad* is to formulate: Agni is the Wind, Agni is the Sun, Agni is the Year. Hence the aim of the whole of Vedic thought may be expressed as the attempt to formulate *upaniṣads*. The texts thus defined, the *Chāndogya* and the *Bṛhadāraṇyaka*, which date from the end of the Vedic period, are far from undermining the speculations of the hymns and the *Brāhmaṇas*; in fact they carry them to their logical conclusion. The Vedic and the Upaniṣadic texts both seek the same end, but they use different means. Vedic thought is scientific in character, or perhaps, more accurately, pre-scientific. Its chain of reasoning starts from the *brahmodya*, discussions of the cosmic enigma or *brahman*, in the old sense of the word. The Vedic riddles, as they used to be called, are not the intellectual diversions of ingenious poets, but represent something of far deeper significance.

It would never be my intention to try to find a single key to the interpretation of the Veda. Mythological legend, considered by itself, expresses many widely differing truths. The most expressive of these myths are those which deal in some way with the creation of the universe, the establishment of heaven and earth, the coming of light and the release of the waters. The theme of the struggle with the dragon is connected with this type of myth. The struggle is described in many forms, but most commonly it is superimposed on an older, more abstract theme, that of the victorious hero, usually Vṛtrahan, who overcomes the enemy resistance. The word *vṛtra* used as a neuter noun meant the defences of the enemy; later it came to be used as the name of a demon in the shape of a dragon or a serpent, identified with Ahi. We cannot account etymologically for the existence of a neuter noun *vṛtra*, unless we trace it back to an abstract idea, just as *mitra* was no doubt 'compact' personified, and *varuṇa* was 'the act of covering' or perhaps 'the act of binding together'. These abstract ideas lie behind many instances of hypostatization: the idea of evil is never clearly personified as a major demon, but is represented under the multiple forms of 'hostility', 'violence', 'resistance'. To translate these words as personal names or agent nouns is to do violence to Vedic terminology. Opposing the idea of evil or primitive anarchy there are *numina* who represent the powers of order in their many forms, both static like the *ṛta* or the *dhāman*, and dynamic like the *indriya*, the *tejas* and the *vāja*. These forces, which regulate relationships in the supernatural world rather as *varṇāśrama* regulates human social relationships in classical times, are endowed with life in the myths. We have already seen the importance of *ṛta*; all that is and all that is to be depends ultimately on it. It is the Vedic precursor of the idea later called *dharma*. There is an opposition between *ṛta* and *anṛta*, disorder or falsehood, on the ethical plane, and between *ṛta* and *nirṛti*, dissolution, on the cosmological plane.

The power of the gods is limited by the interplay of these

forces, just as later it is limited by *karman* or *māyā*. Some Vedic writers already feel that the stories told in the myths belong to the realm of *māyā*; the *Śatapatha* says that Indra never really fought; his very existence is sometimes called into question. India has never believed unreservedly in her own fictions.

These cosmic powers, precursors of the *śaktis*, do not constitute a system of clear-cut oppositions. In classical times Śiva, the terrible destroyer, could also be a kindly protector; similarly in the Vedic system, vast spheres of activity are controlled by ambivalent powers. A normally well-disposed divinity may take on a *ghorā tanū*, an awful aspect; Varuṇa is alarmingly liable to assume the aspect of Vṛtra. Any being who is overshadowed, forced to yield his position to a newer god, or who is relegated to the rôle of a father, is apt to become baleful. It sometimes happens that malevolent, demon-like beings, such as Pipru or Namuci, have a well-disposed counterpart. Sometimes the ambivalence is an integral feature of the divinity, as in the case of Rudra, who is, in this respect only, the prefiguration of Śiva: the two figures have nothing else in common. Terms like *manyu*, *ari*, *māyā*, *yakṣa* and so on have two sets of meanings, according to whether they are used of good or evil beings. Thus in the *Avesta* there are two separate series of epithets, one applicable to the *daēva* world and one to the *āhura* world; but in the Veda the series are no longer separate. The background of the hymns is a troubled one, a scene of passionate rivalries and internal struggles, where great dangers have been faced and surmounted; the abandonment of the *surā*, the establishment of universal allegiance to Indra by gods and men alike, the eclipse of Varuṇa, the acceptance of the Aśvins, the advent of Rudra: none of these events could have been accomplished without great upheavals.

Another illustration of this ambivalence is the association of divinities in pairs. This custom did not survive into subsequent stages of Indian religion: the later Harihara is a subordinate figure, lacking consistent treatment. In the Vedic period we find combinations of widely-varying elements, Dyāvāpṛthivī, Mitrāvaruṇau, Indrāgnī, Indrāviṣṇū and so on. These conjunctions do not always reflect the liturgical arrangement, and it would be interesting to find out by what principles they are governed. M. Dumézil has rightly pointed out,[1] developing Bergaigne's theory,[2] that Varuṇa and Mitra represented two complementary aspects of the sovereign power, one magical and terrible in character, the other juridical and benign. In the case of the Aśvins, the divine pair form a single entity in which it is practically impossible to pick out the component elements. The fact that Viṣṇu and Śiva later share in dominating the Indian religious scene may possibly have some foundation in memories of these old Vedic associations.

We have already noticed the remarkable predominance of Indra, who soon eclipses most of the other divinities; the voluntary or forced withdrawal of Varuṇa before his youthful rival can be gathered from the text itself. Vedic myth becomes 'Indraized'; the cult, too, as in the *Rājasūya*, begins to undergo the same transformation. In the other figures of prime importance, such as Agni and Soma, the ritual elements of which they are personifications can still be clearly discerned. No authentic mythical episodes are associated with them; the only legend that might be suggested in this connection, that of the theft of the *soma* by the Gandharva, is derived from an Indo-European story of the abduction of a liquor that gave immortality, in which *soma* has been substituted for the ambrosia of the legend.

The Veda would have been entirely different in form if the battle-myths connected with Indra had not been intro-

[1] In his *Mitra-Varuṇa*.

[2] In the *Religion védique*, especially the beginning of vol. iii.

duced into it; these myths sometimes have a quite un-Indian ring about them and contain tribal names which cannot belong to the Aryan onomastic. The Indra of the Vedas absorbed the substance of other divinities into himself, just as the Kṛṣṇa of a later period absorbed Viṣṇu, or as the Goddess reduced Śiva to the status of *homunculus*. Indra is a hero of ancient times and retains the appearance and characteristics of a hero. Apart from Kṛṣṇa, he is the only Indian god who ever had a childhood, and whose personality and actions betray human elements. Gods gain in importance not by their virtues, but by the extent of the mythology they inspire. If the influence of the Buddha and Mahāvīra, as founders of sects in ancient India, has been too highly assessed, it is because they very early underwent a kind of mythical apotheosis.

II

Vedism: II

IN richness of mythological invention and assured handling of mythical themes, the *Ṛgveda* was destined to have no successor: Vedism is a mythology that is broken off abruptly. The *Atharvaveda*, a collection intended for domestic use and for the performance of magical rites, and as a hymnary with an esoteric cosmogony, either minimizes the importance of the gods or leaves them altogether out of account. The Atharvan 'reform' is comparable in some respects with that of Zarathustra in Iran. The divinities have become merely decorative in function; the activities they preside over are ill-defined; the part they play is sometimes ludicrous. Indra is a shadowy figure of magic; Varuṇa loses his virility. The only mention of most of the gods is a more or less distorted version of something that has come down from the *Ṛgveda*. Mythopoeic activity ceases when the mind turns to magic, for magic establishes a direct contact between the performer and the effect he desires to produce. On the other hand, in the *Atharvaveda* there is a renewed appeal to demoniac forces, whose power, as we have seen, tended to be restricted in the *Ṛgveda*.

The *Brāhmaṇas* show a metamorphosis of a different kind. They certainly create fresh myths, or rather the beginnings of myths, for most of them terminate abruptly. The story of Manu's surviving the deluge was designed to enhance the efficacy of the milk offering; the offering is Manu's daughter and through her Manu engendered the human race. The significance of all this is far from clear.

The ancient rivalries, which are used to such rich effect in the Veda, are now represented by monotonous struggles between Devas and Asuras. Supreme power is now vested in a new figure, namely Prajāpati, who appears as an unimportant tribal chief in a few passages of the *Ṛgveda*. But like all these new gods, Prajāpati is a colourless figure, devoid of legend. His creative or procreative functions drain him of power. All the gods of the *Brāhmaṇas* are more or less exhausted by their functions and tend to lose their virility; their strength is spent, like that of a hunted-down animal. But Prajāpati is something more, or rather, something less: the name is extended to include the *anirukta*, the symbol of the non-defined, the non-determined; his real name is Ka, 'Who?', and the choice of the number that expresses him, 17, has no rational ground. He represents all that is undefined, whatever in the divine sphere is left unexpressed by the series of the recognized divinities. Under another aspect, he is the Sacrifice, and, again, the function of the Sacrifice is to bring together all uncoordinated phenomena and build them up into an organic whole (even though this structure may be only transitory), and make of the *sarvam* a *viśvam*.

It would be unjustifiable to assume that the period of the *Ṛgveda* with its wealth of mythology was followed by a mechanistic and virtually atheist period. It would be more accurate to say that we are henceforth moving on a different plane of thought; a similar contrast will be observable later on, between the prolific legendary material of the *Viṣṇupurāṇa* and the abstract way in which Śaṅkara or Kumārila represents the world of the gods.

In the *Upaniṣads*, the process of eliminating the gods is complete. Mythology is now conceived as a setting for apologues. Thus, in the *Chāndogya*, Indra is a Brahman student committed to a novitiate lasting 101 years. As we have already seen, the Upaniṣadic writers attach the greatest importance to the system of correspondences, which are not conceived as capable of being externalized in forceful imagery, as in the Veda, but rather as tending to be reabsorbed into the impersonal, abstract principle of *brahman*, the latent energy underlying the old enigmatic formulae. The essence of the *Upaniṣads* is *mīmāṃsā*, reflection, as opposed to the intuitive quality of the hymns and the practical-minded elaborations of the *Brāhmaṇas*. In this way the Veda comes full circle and epitomizes the whole course of the evolution of Indian thought.

Some of the Vedic poets long to penetrate the mystery of the ultimate origin of things, and to find out the nature of the supreme reality that lies beyond the world of the gods, for the gods do not help us to perceive it—indeed, they conceal it from us. In its early stages, this kind of speculation draws extensively upon mythology; it might perhaps never have come into being without the stream of images offered by the myths; but in the end it parts company with mythopoeic thought. Cosmogonic themes are not easily combined with legends of the gods. The *Puruṣa*, or primitive giant, really only creates the social structure. Speculative thought at this period does not envisage time and space on a vast scale, as the classical period does. The word *Yuga*, which later designates the cosmic eras, is used only as a term in dice-playing.

The creation is an emanation, a procreation, the act of an artificer or an artist, a sacrifice, a thought: all possibilities are admitted, but none is finally confirmed. The questions of who made the world and the human body are constantly recurring. More and more new terms are suggested to designate the hidden principle of all things, the *turīyaṃ padam*, the *guhyā nāmāni*. These speculations are assiduously pursued in the *Atharvaveda*; it is as though magical methods were thought to be more appropriate to the subject than the usual ceremonies of praise; Time, the

Breath, the Cow, the Cosmic Support (*Skambha*), the Golden Embryo, the *Virāj* and many other things are put forward as suggestions. Less ingenious minds are content to propose the neuter One, or *Ekam*; the plurality of appearances, they say, is due to the action of *visṛṣṭi*, the principle of individual creation.

Sometimes the full possibilities of a speculative theory of the Veda become apparent only in post-Vedic times. M. Filliozat[1] has drawn attention to a Vedic theory that identified breath and wind; the various physiological processes were expressed in terms of the process of breathing, conceived in the likeness of the wind passing through space. In their cosmic aspect, these ideas are of Indo-Iranian provenance: we know that the Iranian Vayu was in some respects a Supreme Being. These speculations were echoed in classical times, and influenced medical theory. There is an underlying thread of ancient Indian pneumatology running through *Yoga*, with its *prāṇāyāma*, and Tantrism, with its upward surge of the *kuṇḍalinī* and its theory of the bodily 'channels'. The equivalence between the *ātman* and the universal soul was accepted the more easily because originally, as etymology and Ṛgvedic usage show, the term *ātman* connoted breath in its association with wind: *ātmā te vātaḥ*, 'thy breath is the wind', says a well-known passage of the *Ṛgveda*, referring to Varuṇa.

Vedic speculation was the work of a small group of daring poets. Garbe,[2] among others, believed that a spirit of revolt against the priests, or at any rate against ritualism, could be discerned in the *Upaniṣads*; but the *Upaniṣads*

[1] Jean Filliozat, 'La force organique et la force cosmique dans la philosophie médicale de l'Inde et dans le Véda', *Revue Philosophique*, 116 (1933), p. 410; *La doctrine classique de la médecine indienne: ses origines et ses parallèles grecs* (Paris, 1949), p. 51.

[2] R. Garbe, 'Die Weisheit des Brahmanen oder des Kriegers?' (an article of 1893 reprinted in *Beiträge zur indischen Kulturgeschichte* (Berlin, 1903), chap. 1.

are in effect only supplements to the *Brāhmaṇas*, intended for advanced pupils who wanted something beyond the formal course of instruction. That is why the teaching of the *Upaniṣads* starts at the point where exegesis stops: the *Chāndogya* takes Brāhmaṇical meditations on melody as its starting-point, the *Bṛhadāraṇyaka* develops the theme of the mystic meaning of the Horse Sacrifice, which was dealt with in the concluding paragraphs of the *Śatapatha-Brāhmaṇa*. They answered the needs of the ascetics and anchorites, for whom a religion of idols and cult-practice was not enough. There is no more opposition between *Upaniṣad* and *Brāhmaṇa* than there is between the first and second *Mīmāṃsā* or between *Sāṃkhya* and *Yoga*.

But let us look once more at the problems of everyday life. If we ask what were the desires of those people of the Vedic age who were neither *kavis* nor *vipras*, the ordinary cult-worshippers, and the patrons who commissioned the sacrifices, both rich and poor, the answer is that they wanted purely material blessings: money, cattle, sons, good health, success in the arts of war and peace, and the full Vedic span of life, which was a hundred years. This utilitarian view of life is like that of primitive Rome: *bubus ut valeant*, said Cato. There is a great contrast between this materialistic outlook and the heights to which contemporary speculation sometimes rose. But in even the most advanced *Upaniṣads* puns, magical formulae and instruction in eugenics are introduced without the slightest preliminary. In short, the public for whom the hymns were written is not at all preoccupied with the hereafter. There can be no greater blessing than never to die; not to escape from rebirth, which was to be the desire of classical India, not even to escape from *punarmṛtyu*, as the *Brāhmaṇas* say, but simply to prolong the present life. Vedic ethics are based on this naïve aspiration, and are mainly concerned with length of days.

Conceptions of the after-life are no less rudimentary. Heaven, which lies at the highest point of the firmament, consists of material pleasure; it is a paradise of light; it is more beautiful than the earth because, we are told, there are more nights there. It is sometimes spoken of with a kind of intoxication, as in the blessed visions of Indra, when he is exalted by the *soma*. Sometimes the other world was conceived of as the realm of Yama, lying beneath the earth. But this conception soon fell into disfavour because of the natural aversion in which all things subterranean are held and the fact that, although the Veda gives no clear idea of the infernal regions, they are thought of as a black hole. Hence Yama, formerly the ruler of paradise, is abruptly transformed into the king of the infernal world. It is clear, in short, that the Veda offers only the slightest of precedents for the preoccupation with eschatology that characterizes Hinduism, Buddhism and Jainism.

The same may be said of the theories of transmigration, *saṃsāra*, and the future retribution of earthly actions, *karman*. There is no clear trace of the former theory; and the latter theory appears only in the primitive conception that good deeds are rewarded by a life of bliss, the *sukṛta* or the *sukṛtasya lokaḥ*, evil deeds by a life of torment, *duṣkṛta* or *duryoṇa*. Sylvain Lévi, with some degree of exaggeration, described the attitude of the *Brāhmaṇas* as amoral.[1] For these writers, the essential is to perform the prescribed action, the *kriyā* or *karman*, with scrupulous exactitude. *Śraddhā* is in effect only the confidence that one has in the efficacy of the action; the old term *ṛta*, with its wide range of associations, has been replaced by *satya*, which means exactitude. There are isolated passages in the *Upaniṣads* in which the word *karman* is used in the sense of a good or bad action on the moral plane; but it is never used for the present effect of a past action or the foreseeable consequence

[1] *La doctrine du sacrifice dans les Brāhmaṇas* (Paris, 1898), esp. p. 9.

of an action performed in the present, conceptions which constitute the essential meaning of the word in later usage. Vedic determinism is confined to ritual. Even the frequently cited passage, *BĀU.* III, 2, 13, does not imply that the writer was acquainted with the principle of systematic retribution.

But Vedic religion is first and foremost a liturgy, and only secondarily a mythological or speculative system; we must therefore investigate it as a liturgy. In its principal treatises we have a collection unparalleled in antiquity; they describe every operation, every gesture of the Vedic ritual appropriate to each ceremony, each officiant and each school. I cannot here go into the interesting question of the schools, for that would be to embark on problems that still await solution. A philological comparison of all the sources would probably enable us to reconstruct a primitive form of ritual something like that prevailing in the Ṛgvedic period; at present we only have the separate recensions of groups that date from different periods and that have long been widely dispersed.

The Vedic rites are made to conform to a systematic arrangement; mythology may be lacking in system, but ritual is overburdened with it. It appears that originally separate rites were grouped together in vast systems in response to new demands that had arisen in the course of time, and under the influence of an advancing scholasticism. There is a distinction between the great public rites, called *Śrauta*, and the domestic rites, called *Gṛhya.* The former are carried out by professional officiants, and need three fires; the formulary is taken from the *Saṃhitā.* The domestic rites take place on the family hearth, and are performed by the householder, using a formulary taken from a special collection. The two series are entirely different in character, in spite of the resemblances that arise from borrowings. The Indians, with their taste for classification, divide the solemn rites into seven *saṃsthās* or ordinary celebrations, with vegetable and animal offerings, and seven others, based on the *soma* oblations. But the *soma* sacrifices necessitate ordinary vegetable and animal oblations, and the *Sautrāmaṇī* involves milk, *surā* and a sacrificial victim. The tendency to build up complex structures from simpler elements is illustrated by the fact that some sacrifices, all using a common *tantra*, are variations of a single archetype. Some festivals, such as the *sattras* or 'sessions', are too complicated to be actually carried out, and are intended rather as intellectual exercises. It is clear that the texts contain a proportion of such exercises; we must not regard them as consisting entirely of accounts of actual religious practice.

I do not intend to engage in a theoretical consideration of the nature of the ritual. Ritual has a strong attraction for the Indian mind, which tends to see everything in terms of formulae and methods of procedure, even when such adjuncts no longer seem really necessary for its religious experience. When Naciketas, the young Brahman, who has visited the realm of the dead, tells the god Yama of his desire to know whether or not man lives on after death, the god's only resource is to advise him to set up a 'Fire'. All the great mysteries are revealed to the man who knows how to pile up the bricks of the Fire-Altar and make the right offerings on it. There are no personal prayers, uttered spontaneously, in either the Vedic or the Classical periods. The ceremonies of religion take place on the days assigned to them in the calendar, daily, fortnightly, or at certain seasons. There is provision for votive rites, *Kāmyeṣṭis*, to obtain special favours, but they are only the ordinary procedures with the addition of a votive formula. In the same way an operation can be adapted, with only slight changes, for use as an act of expiation.

The most imposing ceremonies, which may also be the

oldest, the *Rājasūya*, the *Aśvamedha* and the *Vājapeya*, are reserved for princes: they are rare and costly occasions, which were a pretext for lavish celebrations, like potlatches in character, which are carefully recorded in classical inscriptions. It is proposed to reconstruct one of these great sacrifices, the *Vājapeya*, at Poona in the near future; this should be an event of great interest to Vedic scholars.

There are various types of ritual, then, designed for different purposes. The most solemn forms are preceded by a characteristic ceremony, the consecration or *dīkṣā*; this may be based on the private ceremonial that takes place at the beginning of a Brahman student's career, for it has many analogies with it. Both ceremonies have the same object: to raise the participant from the sphere of the profane to that of the sacred (a process of *dūrohaṇa*, painful ascent) by freeing him from worldly vices, as Mauss said.[1] At the end of the ceremonial, the reverse process, *avabhṛtha*, or descent from the sacred sphere, takes place; and the consecrated objects are carried away by flowing water.

This practice thus centres round the patron of the sacrifice, the layman who pays for the ceremony and receives its spiritual benefits. It is interesting to note that the layman himself, with his wife, takes his place among the officiants, though his is not a very active rôle; he has no hieratic formulary at his disposal, as the professionals have. But his presence is essential; he recites some of the prayers, and may even replace one of the officiants on occasion; Yājñavalkya was led to protest at his encroachments at one stage. It must not be forgotten that at all periods the service of the temples, or at any rate their administration, could be entrusted to the laymen, and that the *Smṛti* includes among the rights of the *kṣatriya* and even of the

[1] H. Hubert and M. Mauss, 'Essai sur la nature et la fonction du sacrifice', *Année Sociologique*, 2 (1898), p. 52.

vaiśya that of 'sacrificing for his own benefit'. The wife plays a very subordinate part, but all the same she is there, a silent participant who occasionally has an action to perform, as when, in the *Vājapeya*, the husband and wife climb on to the post that is surmounted by the solar wheel. This may be a reflection of the low esteem in which woman was held in Vedic India, as some of Yājñavalkya's remarks seem to suggest. Women are often introduced in licentious rôles, as in the Horse Sacrifice, when the queen has to lie beside the slaughtered horse, and in the *Varuṇapraghāsas*, when the priest asks her, 'How many lovers have you?' and she has to answer by holding up as many blades of grass as the number of lovers she admits to having. There is a foreshadowing of the drama in this scene, as there is elsewhere in the Vedic ritual and hymns, especially the famous dialogues of the *Ṛgveda* which accompany or replace some kind of passage in mime. There is no doubt but that the cult contained an element of the drama: in classical times pilgrimages were enlivened by portrayals of the deeds of Rāma and Kṛṣṇa, and the Bengali *yātrās* include plays and farces.

The number of officiants varies: the main responsibility rests on the *adhvaryu*, who is in charge of 'ways and means' and who performs various actions, moves about and recites at considerable length in a low tone. The *hotṛ*, who, as the etymology of the word suggests, was originally the libation-pourer, later becomes primarily a reciter; but his invocations, which are said aloud, impressive though they are, play only a small part in the liturgy as a whole, rather like the music of the chanters. The *brahman*, who, as his name reminds us, is the repository of the unexpressed power of the formula, is a silent spectator, whose duty it is to see that the operation is carried out with accuracy; he is a professional expert, like the Roman priest. His silence is just as valuable as the speech and melodies of his colleagues.

The complex system of sixteen or seventeen officiants was a later development of the simpler form that appears in the *Ṛgveda*; here eight names are mentioned in all, those of seven officiants and the *yajamāna*, then called the 'householder'. The functions assumed by these seven officiants, headed by the *hotṛ*, connected each of them with one particular god; this was known as *ṛtu*, in the old sense of the word, the connection between sacerdotal function and tutelary deity: the *hotṛ* and the *brahman* were associated with Indra, the *adhvaryu* (or both *adhvaryus*) with the Aśvins, the *praśāstṛ* with Varuṇa, the *agnidh* with Agni, the *neṣṭṛ* with Tvaṣṭṛ, the *potṛ* with the Maruts.

The *Ṛgveda* mentions a presser, who took part in the less complex festivals. This function could be performed by the layman, for at this early period the pressing of *soma* was also carried out for domestic purposes, with a pestle and mortar. The growth of the *soma* cult may bear some relationship to the expansion of Indra's rôle. In that case, the oblations that involved bloodshed may have been part of the cult of Varuṇa, the supreme and terrible god: they were introduced at intervals in the somic ceremony. Finally, of the purely vegetable oblations, some were offered to the gods who protected the harvest, like Pūṣan, some to those who watched over contracts, like Mitra, some to yet other gods.

It must also be remembered that there were no temples at the Vedic period: 'the sacrifice takes place within the officiants themselves', says one of the *Brāhmaṇas*. The term *āyatana*, which later came to mean 'sanctuary', merely designates the ordinary domestic hearth in Vedic times. The temple cult of the classical period must have grown out of the domestic cult. Sacrifices took place on a specially prepared piece of ground, but the same spot was not necessarily used again for subsequent ceremonies. There was no building other than temporary huts, constructed on a framework of poles joined together at the top by transverse beams, and roofed over with thatching. The instruments used were also rather rudimentary, though their functions were highly specialized: there was a whole set of spoons, cauldrons and other receptacles, and for the kindling of fire the ancient method of the tourniquet-wheel was still used; there were peculiar shards, pieces of brick or earthenware perhaps, arranged in the shape of a horse-shoe, on which the paste was placed to cook over the embers. The centre of the sacred ground is called the *vedi*: it was sometimes a raised mound, but more often a pit made to receive the oblations and the various instruments, thus expressing the invitation to the gods in concrete form.

It is impossible to describe the procedure in detail. Several scholars have given general descriptions of it, notably A. B. Keith.[1] The individual features of the ritual could only be explained by invoking the same principle of esotericism by which we are guided in any attempt at interpreting the mythical narratives of the Veda. In any case, one cannot grasp even the outward meaning from reading the text by itself unless one is gifted with the rare virtuosity of a Caland. It would be necessary to follow several scores, as it were, at the same time, and to bear in mind the various formularies from which the recitations and chants are drawn, seemingly at random. The best way to understand the nature of these ceremonies is to be a spectator at one of them as they are still enacted to this day throughout India —in a spirit of historical reconstruction rather than from religious motives, I should imagine, though one can never be sure.

I recently had the opportunity of seeing one of these

[1] Cf. *The Religion and Philosophy of the Veda* (op. cit.). Also A. Hillebrandt, *Ritual-Litteratur: Vedische Opfer und Zauber* (Strassburg, 1897). A more recent account is that of P. V. Kane, *History of Dharmaśāstra* (Poona, 1930 etc.), esp. vol. 2, part 2 (1941).

ceremonies myself: it was a fairly simple one, a *Darśapūrṇamāsa* performed according to the *Hairaṇyakeśa* recension. It took place at Poona, under the supervision of a Vedic Institute. It was a convincing, and, as far as one could tell, a faithful reproduction, although there was some inevitable simplification and several deviations, of which some compared more favourably than others with the ancient model. The age of the *paddhatis* and *prayogas* had obviously intervened. One did, however, derive from it an understanding of the nature and the *raison d'être* of the various prescriptions, movements and gestures. This type of ceremony is much more spectacular than the classical cult with its mumbled prayers and its noisy offering of oblations round the idol. In those distant days India had a feeling for liturgy comparable to that of the Roman Church.

The significance of certain movements prescribed in the ritual depends on their connection with other actions. Those that constitute the introduction to the oblation are of this kind; a serpentine advance, or *prasarpaṇa*, winding in and out to the accompaniment of invocations, is a characteristic feature of the processional entry to the *sadas*: the officiants proceed in single file, each one holding the shoulders of the man in front; they walk bent forward, sliding their feet and licking their lips. This is because it is the morning pressing that is taking place, and the sacrifice has yet to increase. At the midday pressing, they walk upright, but still with their heads bowed; only in the evening are their heads raised.

The ritual is devised not only to dignify and strengthen the corresponding secular procedures, but also as the symbolic expression of speculative theory. Perhaps we shall never know for certain whether speculative thought dictated the form of the ritual, or whether, as seems generally more likely, speculation was a later development. But the fact remains that in many cases an action is closely bound up with its esoteric significance. For the *Caru* oblation, the officiant hollows out a depression in the middle of the paste, pours liquid butter into it and looks for his reflection in it, as in a mirror. If his reflection does not appear, he repeats the process of pouring in butter. If the reflection still fails to appear, it is a sign that his life is drawing to a close. This appears to be a magical rite that has found its way into the ceremony; it is sometimes used to find out whether a sick man will recover or not. But as Vedic religion is consciously optimist and maintains that no action is inexpiable, the danger can be averted by anointing the eyes with the butter, and by beseeching King Soma to whom the cake is dedicated: 'It is thou who touchest the heart (i.e. who healest it by thy touch); it is thou who givest a healthy colour; give me a healthy colour!' Such episodes are much more interesting than the endless sequence of oblations, punctuated by the harsh shout of '*svāhā!*' when the liquid jet touches the flame and makes it leap up.

Other rites are really independent scenes which have become associated with the ceremony, such as the dice-playing scene at the beginning of the Royal Consecration, the race of seventeen chariots in the *Vājapeya*, the selling of *soma* at the beginning of the *Agniṣṭoma*, and the occasional introduction of profane music. The profane is very close to the sacred in many of these scenes, as even a very superficial knowledge of the society and everyday life of the time is enough to show us. The buying of *soma* is obviously an imitation of a custom obtaining in commercial practice. The *adhvaryu* arranges the plants on a red bullock-skin: he then hands them to the make-believe merchant: 'Seller of *soma*, have you any *soma* to sell?' 'Yes.' 'From Mount Mūjavant?' (From the *Ṛgveda* onwards, it was considered that the best *soma* grew on Mount Mūjavant.) 'Yes.' 'I will buy some from you for the upper part of this cow's foot—for half its foot—for the whole foot. Well, then, for a quarter of the animal.' But the merchant is still not satisfied, and says, 'What else will you give in exchange?' 'Here is gold, here is a goat, here is a garment.' Needless to say, each of these objects has a symbolic significance. The merchant is punished for his tenacity: there is a pretence of strangling him and of blinding him; his precious merchandise is taken from him by force; he is driven away with blows. This would not be surprising if the merchant were a *śūdra* or a member of the despised family of Kautsas. The whole scene may have been intended to convey the illegality of trading in *soma*.

Certain rites give us an insight into a god's nature. In the *Sākamedhas* there is a funeral ceremony which includes an offering to Rudra; at the conclusion of the ceremony the remains of the oblation are put into two baskets which are hung one at each end of a beam, out of the reach of the oxen: this is a viaticum offered to Rudra to persuade him to go away without doing harm. M. Dumézil has drawn attention to an episode in the Royal Consecration,[1] in which, according to the commentaries at least, the new king loses his virility at a decisive moment in the ceremony; he must regain it by precipitating himself on a herd of cows belonging to one of his near relations. In this way Varuṇa himself once lost his virility when he was consecrated king. This episode may be compared with the well-known story of how Ouranos, who persecuted his own family, was castrated by one of them. Admittedly, the analogy is not exact, but there are many parallels between the two episodes which provide some foundation for a comparison.

Other episodes are more closely connected with speculative thought. Among these is the *pravargya*, with its oblationary vessel called *mahāvīra*, 'the great man', which is worshipped, and considered to be the 'head of the sacrifice'. It is associated with the demon Makha, the

[1] *Ouranos-Varuṇa* (op. cit.), p. 72.

malevolent counterpart of Viṣṇu, who was beheaded by the gods. Here, as on other occasions, it is not fortuitous that ritual emphasizes that the gods can be made to suffer: the imagination looses divine forces, but human action can reabsorb or control them. The *Sautrāmaṇī* is more elaborate. Rönnow believed that the myth of the demon Namuci could be traced in the general outlines of this ceremony[1] (and tradition supports the theory); the *Ṛgveda* has not much to say of Namuci, but later texts tell us that he concluded an imprudent pact with Indra, according to which he should not suffer death under any foreseeable circumstances, and that Indra beheads him in the half-light with the foam of the waves. But it is not admissible that the associated liturgy could have been similarly inspired, for it is on entirely different lines.

The Fire-Altar in particular, a brick construction in the shape of a bird, has been the subject of a great deal of speculation. It was ancillary to many other ceremonies; the concluding stages of cult ceremonial centred round it; it was the apogee of the religious drama. It is Prajāpati who is sacrificed and dismembered, as was the primeval man, the *Puruṣa*, in the *Ṛgveda*. The god is then restored in the form of the altar, which is the representation in space (as M. Mus observed[2]) of an abstract religious conception of duration. As Prajāpati is in fact the sacrifice, the altar also symbolizes the combining of scattered and anarchical elements into the organic structural norm which will henceforth ensure the ordered functioning of the universe.

As these examples show, the texture of Vedic ritual is very rich. Elemental forces play as great a part in it as abstraction and speculation. We can see in it the reflection,

[1] 'Zur Erklärung des Pravargya, des Agnicayana und der Sautrāmaṇī', *Monde Orient.*, 23, p. 113.

[2] 'Le Barabuḍur', *Bull. Éc. franç. Extr.-Orient*, 32 ff. (1932 etc.), introduction, *passim.*

however distorted, of a society, with its customs and amusements, its court life and its humble callings, and its background of husbandry and stock-rearing following their seasonal rhythm.

The domestic rites are often more closely related to everyday life, since they are enacted inside the house, without any public audience or ceremonial setting. They are of two kinds. Some are short daily practices, formulae accompanying some simplified form of oblation. The other rites are more characteristic; taken together they constitute the *saṃskāras*, that is, the dedications by which the individual gradually approaches the state of the 'twice-born', reaches it, and is confirmed in the privilege. In this way all the most important phases of human existence are covered, from birth and before until death and beyond. The oblation plays only a secondary rôle, or is omitted altogether. On the other hand, the idea of impurity, which is only partially attested in the public ritual, appears very clearly; this is another respect in which the domestic rite shows itself to be the forerunner of the religious practices and conceptions of classical India.

But, as has already been pointed out, the Vedic element in these rites is very slight. The formulae alone give evidence of hieratic inspiration, and even then, those borrowed from the *Ṛgveda* stand out clearly as interpolations at various points. This religion is really Hinduism, and even at times an anticipation of Tantrism. Part of the ceremonial dedicated to the Manes was incorporated into the public ritual, among the four-monthly offerings or among those of the new moon and the full moon; but some of the practices can also be carried out at the 'domestic' level. The fact that in the *Ṛgveda*, and to a greater extent in the *Atharva*, there are wedding and funeral prayers that have slipped in under cover of praise of the gods, shows that those who composed the hymns were not indifferent to the events of domestic life: it is not impossible that there existed a small domestic *Saṃhitā* which may have been later absorbed into the composite collection that constitutes the tradition of the Atharvāṅgiras.

There are many forms of initiation: forms for the dedication of the young Brahman student, for marriage, and even for funeral practices. They too, apparently, are derived from the public ritual, which has influenced the actions and the form of words: this is a process which might be termed the 'Vedicization' of private ritual. On the other hand, all the agricultural rites seem to have been private in origin. But we cannot come to any definite decision on such problems when we are dealing with an evolutionary process of which we know only the most recent stages.

Expiatory practices play a considerable part. We come across them scattered throughout the treatises on solemn ceremonial practice as well as the others. They inspired a new type of literature, also superficially Vedic in form, the *Dharmasūtras*, in which the theory of expiation is expounded together with a rudimentary form of law teaching. It was in this way that religious conceptions achieved a position among the rules which were being laboriously evolved to define the legal status of the citizen and his duties in society.

Lastly, there is the magical element. Ritual in general abounds in operations based on magic, and it is well known that there is no radical separation between the two realms. But normal cult-practice follows the lines already laid down for it by rigorous tradition. Magic seems to be invented specially for each case as it arises. It is free of any connection with the priesthood and with society and its organization: it is a transaction that takes place between the man who seeks its help for his own purposes and the sorcerer, who has no official title, but is accorded the name of *purohita* when his client is a prince and he is acting in an official capacity. The procedure of magic is based on more or less arbitrary and sometimes esoteric prescriptions for obtaining possession of something or for compelling some result to happen. The formula fits the action more exactly than in any other field; the action translates the formula and gives it life. Imitative practices are very common. To change the course of a river, reeds are planted and a frog with green stripes is placed on the ground; as Oldenberg said,[1] the method is to make a simulacrum of the life of the river-bed along the course that one wishes the river to take, and the reality will follow.

It is curious that magic, like private cult-practice, finds its way into the public ceremonial. Part of one of the Vedas, the *Atharvaveda*, is devoted to it; it is true that this is a late work that is not accepted as authentic in its entirety and does not properly conform to ancient hieraticism. Another Veda, the *Sāmaveda*, gave rise to magical practices by reason of the incantatory character that was early attributed to the *sāmans*. Magic also left its mark in the *Brāhmaṇas*, one of which, the *Sāmavidhāna*, is given up to it. In this way, by a sort of agreed fiction, a large number of magical practices are included in the description of the new moon and full moon sacrifices. Sometimes a minute alteration in the liturgy is all that is needed to transform an ordinary action into *abhicāra*. The remains of the consecrated oblation can be used, for example, to anoint the object to which the magical action is directed.

These acts, taken as a whole, are anarchical in character. Stable order is entirely lacking. Like other forms of religion in India, Vedism thus becomes debased to the level of somewhat crude witchcraft. In the *Upaniṣads*, ritualism goes to the opposite extreme, and is sublimated into abstract speculation: but in the process there is the

[1] *Die Religion des Veda* (op. cit.), p. 507.

risk that it will be destroyed or laughed to scorn, as in the passage where the *Muṇḍaka* waxes ironical on the subject of those 'frail craft', the eighteen forms of the sacrifice. But the *Upaniṣads* themselves, or at any rate the two earliest ones, contain a certain amount of crude and childish material, as we have already seen. Extremes meet in India.

It is difficult to sum up the general impression that the Veda makes on us; in many respects it is a strange and even monstrous testimony; the utmost caution must be exercised in using it as material for any subject not directly envisaged by it, whether it be linguistics, sociology, the history of religion or ethnography. We must approach it dispassionately, putting aside all the absurd and untenable theses to which many researchers, in the West as well as in the East, have subscribed. Again, we must always bear in mind the pitfalls into which we should be led by blindly following tradition, which, venerable though it may be, has now, it must be admitted, largely lost its feeling for the living reality represented by the old texts, and supplies the deficiency by a kind of intuitional approach based on memories of a much more recent period. We must not forget that there is a gap of twenty-five or thirty centuries between Sāyaṇa and the hymns, and we are conscious that the tradition that connects them is an interrupted one.

The importance of the Veda to India is well known. Its imprint on Hinduism is permanent and unmistakable; and on Buddhism and Jainism, too, it has left a deep impression, if only in the reaction it produced in them. It seems likely that many Indian literary disciplines would have developed quite differently if there had not originally been that striking sequence of hymns, commentaries, descriptive aphorisms and philosophoumena, which were drawn upon and imitated over so long a period. Vedism is a religion, but it is even more a technique; a technique of learned poets and erudite theologians, which has given rise to the most atheistic of the philosophical systems of Brahmanical India, the *Mīmāmṣā*; the *Mīmāṃsā* only develops the thought of the *Brāhmaṇas*; it is the jurisprudence of the ritual act. The definitions, logical argument and interpretative maxims elaborated by the *Mīmāṃsā* for students of the old public ceremonial were so highly considered that they were taken over into other fields, notably the *Dharmaśāstra*. Thus, throughout the Middle Ages, we see the legal commentaries floundering on rules that had been drawn up to meet the needs of a sacrifice long fallen into desuetude.

Vedism even developed the secular disciplines, phonetics and grammar, astronomy, the rudiments of law, even geometry, because its teaching made use of them. In the *Nighaṇṭus*, probably the oldest lexicon in any Indo-European language, words are grouped as series of synonyms. These synonyms are mostly secondary, metaphorical acceptations of the words, in accordance with the laws of occult correlations and equivalences of which we have already spoken; and it is this type of symbolical synonymics, as it might be called, that reappears in the lexica of the classical period, in the commentaries and in the very phraseology of many of the *kāvyas*.

Let us consider a few instances of Vedic survivals, chosen more or less at random. It is claimed that the *Pañcarātra* system is founded on the Veda, that it belongs to a school of the *Yajurveda*, the *Ekāyana*; the school is unknown to us, but it is possible that there is some recollection of it in a passage of the *Chāndogya* (VII, 1, 2). The Vedic *Vaikhānasa* school was continued by a Vaiṣṇavite *Saṃhitā* of the same name, dating from a late period, which preserves a complete fire ritual. The school of medicine evidenced by the manual known as the *Kāśyapa-Saṃhitā* endeavours to reproduce the *Brāhmaṇa* style, which seems to indicate a desire to emphasize its connection with Vedism. Some of the later sects, like the Nātha Siddhas, which adopt a Tantric *Yoga*, have re-established a *soma* cult, though in symbolic rather than concrete form. A late Buddhist text, the *Tattvasaṃgraha*, gives evidence of a Vedic school, the *Nimittaśākhā*, of which nothing has come down to us from any other source. An earlier text, the *Vajrasūcī* attributed to Aśvaghoṣa, contains quotations from the Veda. A text of Jaina inspiration, the *Yaśastilaka*, in polemizing against the Brahmanic cult, gives some curious details about the Veda and the old sacrifices.

We are quite uninformed about some aspects of Vedism. Of religious feeling and community life in the Vedic period we can know virtually nothing. The schools, as we call them, are known to us only by their recensions. We are constantly having to make inferences about religious phenomena from philological evidence.

It would seem that whatever survived of Vedism has become so integral a part of Indian thought that it is no longer distinguishable as a separate element. The rest died out, as did the conception of the god Varuṇa: today we have to look to the extreme limit of Indian expansion, the island of Bali, to find a temple dedicated to him. Yet the recitation of the hymns is still practised, and I do not think it is a case of purely formal adherence to an extinct tradition. It is amazing to see that even to the present day there are men living in the uttermost parts of India, who have never met one another, and who yet, in their recitation or chanting of the Veda, carry out the infinitely subtle processes of a consummate analytical technique with complete accuracy of memory. If the principal texts were lost, they could be reconstituted, thanks to these men.

India in her exhaustion has often taken refuge in *ahiṃsā* and the Vedāntic scale of values; but a new and more self-assertive generation may be at hand, a generation imbued with the spirit of Yājñavalkya who, when he was asked if he permitted the eating of meat, replied, 'Yes, as long as it is tender. . . .' The Veda may once again become a great source of inspiration, as it was to the fiery Dayānanda Sarasvatī in the nineteenth century, who set out to establish a mystique of national and social import based on the Vedas.

As a source of academic interest for the scholar, the Veda is by no means exhausted: but let us in conclusion very briefly consider its value as literature. In the nineteenth century it was the fashion to deride the '*galimatias védique*', as Bergaigne called it;[1] Max Müller said that one could not read ten pages of *Brāhmaṇa* without revulsion;[2] and Von Schroeder likened the formulae of the *Yajurveda* to the ravings of mental delirium.[3] The *Upaniṣads* escaped attack because India's contributions to speculative thought are always treated with respect. But the prose-style of the *Śatapatha* is a model of skilful articulation, and in its severe purity reminds us of Plato. There is a strangeness of expression in the hymns which we may well find compelling now that our standards of poetry are more flexible, and our ideal is an art that combines the primitive with the elaborate.

[1] Esp. in his article 'Quelques observations sur les figures de rhétorique dans le Ṛig-Veda', *Mém. Soc. Lin.*, 4, p. 96.

[2] *Chips from a German Workshop* (London, 1867, vol. i; later editions 1868 etc.).

[3] Leopold von Schroeder, *Indiens Literatur und Cultur in historischer Entwicklung* (Leipzig, 1887), p. 113.

III

Hinduism: I

THE long succession of religious developments which followed Vedism cannot be easily grouped. It is sometimes proposed to divide them into an older period, which would be designated as 'brāhmanism', during which the main trend is towards uniformity rather than sectarianism, and a later period, when sects abound, which would be that of Hinduism proper. But the sects are certainly older than literary evidence shows; the Tantric aspect, as it is called, which after a certain period is characteristic of the greater part of religious practices, also has origins far back in the past. The same may be said of *bhakti*. If we confine our search to the origins of religious phenomena, we tend to overlook the fact that India is constantly contributing new material, or revivifying the old; if, on the other hand, we concentrate too closely on one particular stage of religious development, we may err in assuming that the facts we are studying are without roots in the past. In India everything is in one sense older, and in another sense of more recent origin than is generally supposed.

If we wished to attempt a definition and classification of the essentials of Indian religion we could take as our starting-point religion as it is today, with its multiplicity of local cults, beliefs and superstitions, and its many village gods, and try to compare it with what we know of the ancient religion from literary and archaeological evidence; and we could then consider it in relationship to forms of religion outside India. This method would inevitably result in a collection of miscellaneous features which would be conveniently termed 'non-Aryan', or perhaps, less cautiously, 'Dravidian' or 'pre-Aryan', and which would really be features common to primitive religions all over the world. What would remain then as a basis for 'classical' Hinduism? Nothing, apart from those elements emanating from Vedism; and we must bear in mind that Vedism itself contains elements of primitive religion, and therefore of Hinduism (or, we might say, of pre-Hinduism), the existence of which at a period earlier than the Veda could be verified by the evidence of the Mohenjo-Daro excavations.

The Vedic contribution to Hinduism, especially to Hindu cult-practice and speculation, is not a large one; Vedic influence on mythology is rather stronger, though here also there has been a profound regeneration. Religious terminology is almost completely transformed between the Veda and the Epic or the *Purāṇas*, a fact which has not been sufficiently emphasized; the old terms have disappeared or have so changed in meaning that they are hardly recognizable; a new terminology comes into being. Even in those cases where continuity has been suggested, as for Rudra-Śiva, the differences are really far more striking than the similarities. It has been claimed, on grounds that do not seem altogether unreasonable, that Śiva is a figure of Dravidian origin. The same claim has been made, though less categorically, even for Viṣṇu, who appears in the hymns as a minor divinity. An Eurasian provenance for the Great Goddess has been put forward as a possibility (even if she already appears in the Veda under the name of Aditi), and it has been suggested that Indra owes his origin to Asia Minor. Similarly, *Yoga* and even *Sāṃkhya* have been accounted for in terms of primitive Asiatic features. It would have been quicker to enumerate those elements that are demonstrably Aryan: they would consist of perhaps a few functional gods (as it is the fashion to describe them), the *soma* cult and the rudiments of a social system: little enough, in all conscience.

I believe that these theories are exaggerated, and that they are based on superficial explanations. The empty terms 'non-Aryan' and 'primitive' are used too readily; in seeking to prove too much, one runs the risk of finally proving nothing but the obvious fact that Hinduism possesses the morphological and typological features common to all forms of religion at a certain stage of development. It must always be borne in mind that Hinduism is the expression of a great civilization and is closely connected with philosophical speculation and literary activity, and that it is a product of the creative imagination and a systematic construction.

Its sources are enormous, and consist of a great variety of texts written in many dialects. There is hardly an Indian language, from Sanskrit down to those of most recent development, which has not been used to express religious conceptions, usually before being used for many other purposes. The slow and obscure beginnings of Sanskrit as a secular language are well known; other dialects underwent the same process. It has been constantly asserted that India is obsessed with religion. It might be equally well maintained that India takes no cognizance of religion, at least as an independent phenomenon. Religion is not conceived as a duty, or as a problem facing every human being on reaching maturity. It is a heritage and a tradition. The only word which expresses it is *dharma*, which in the Veda designated certain standards applying particularly to the world of the gods. The term includes not only religion but all the ethical, social and legal principles associated with religion, and which together with it constitute the real meaning of life for the Hindu. The word is so wide in meaning that Rādhākṛṣṇan can only define it as 'right conduct'.

Hinduism is not built on any Canon or Gospel, and (I suppose as a necessary corollary) it has no founder or dogma. The earliest available text, the *Mahābhārata*, which is rightly regarded as a *summa* of ancient Hinduism, devotes no special attention to religion, even in its didactic passages. Its inspiration is fundamentally secular; its task is to focus attention on a certain type of man, the *Kṣatriya*. The *Laws of Manu* provide a good illustration of the interlacing of themes in Indian literature: here we have a legislative text, or at any rate a book of legal maxims, which begins with an account of the creation of the world, and ends with an exposition of the future consequences of earthly actions, the nature of the soul and the path of Liberation: nothing could better illustrate the interdependence of all spheres of human activity. If we trace the development of *Smṛti* from its origins, we can see how criminal law gradually grew out of the theory of expiation, and how civil law itself hewed out a path from ritual prescriptions.

If the Epic was intended for the edification of princes, the *Purāṇas* seem to be specifically religious texts; they claim to be divinely inspired, 'promulgated by Viṣṇu, by Śiva or Brahman'; but this means little in India, where every important text claims a divine origin. The *Purāṇas* are a store-house of myths and legends; together with the *Harivaṃśa*, they are the principal source of Hindu mythology. They contain descriptions of religious practices and sanctuaries; they are the handbooks of the pilgrim. But they are also what we should call works of popular science dealing with cosmogony and genealogies of dynasties. Their aim is to show how the reigning dynasties and the dynasties to come (for there is a prophetic part, written, as might be expected, *a posteriori*) are linked with the dynasties of the past, back to the earliest days of myth. The *Purāṇas* even treat of grammar, poetics, and other secular disciplines, as did the Vedic writings.

It would have been easier to enumerate the texts devoid of reference to religion: here there is a contrast with Greece, where religious literature is practically non-existent. It is not by chance that no original treatise on *Lokāyata*, the once flourishing materialistic school, has come down to us. Everything which did not conform to certain standards disappeared. Of the ancient theatre only the noble *genres* have survived, with rare exceptions. The *Arthaśāstra* of Kauṭilya, an essentially secular politico-economic treatise, passes for an inspired text: it begins with a divine genealogy and ends with magical formulae which are included, and not fortuitously, under the heading *upaniṣad*.

Fundamentally, religious books can be defined as books written for the use of a sect, like the Vaiṣṇavite *Saṃhitās*, the Śaivite *Āgamas*, and the *Tantras* proper. They proclaim a new law, the *tāntriko vidhiḥ*, as opposed to the *vaidiko vidhiḥ*; even the term *tāntrikā śrutiḥ* is found. They are manuals, or if they were not so long I should say breviaries, expressing definite conceptions. At this period, which we may assume, as a hypothesis, to be the seventh century, the great religious ideas have already been expressed several times. It follows that religious literature in India is a literature of reformation. We never see the first stages or the foundation of a movement. It is a literature of an anonymous and apocryphal nature: the first author to whom a definite date can be assigned seems to be Jayadeva in the twelfth century.

In these circumstances, it is not surprising that Hinduism sought its inspiration in the Vedic *Upaniṣads*. Hence its ceaseless efforts to compose new *Upaniṣads*, down to the sixteenth century at least. These little treatises, however, were scarcely suitable for their rôle: they look back to the past; and they are the outcome of an academic preoccupation with a kind of meta-ritualism. They have scientific pretensions, as we have already seen. The great classical themes, *Saṃsāra*, *Karman*, the techniques of mysticism, the problems of asceticism, are practically unknown to them. In short, although we must acknowledge the great contribution made by the *Upaniṣads* in directing Hindu doctrine towards monism (for without their influence, India might perhaps have gone over to dualism and have adopted the doctrine of *anātmatva*, like the Buddhists) it must be admitted that they could have exerted no direct influence on religious manifestations. The Veda is venerated from a distance, but it is hardly drawn upon at all.

There remains the *Bhagavadgītā*, which has been called the Gospel of Kṛṣṇa. This composite text, taken from the Great Epic, expounds several teachings simultaneously; it became the principal guide of many Indians just as the *Bhāgavatapurāṇa*, the *summa* of Kṛṣṇaism, was later to become, and as, later still, the *Rāmāyaṇa* of Tulsīdās, the synthesis of Rāmaism, was to be in Northern India. Śaivism has nothing corresponding to these works. But they are all, including the *Gītā*, not so much new messages as summaries of earlier teachings, and we can still discern in them the ill-assorted elements from which the structure was built up.

In order to write a detailed history of Hinduism, every sort of evidence would have to be considered: the task has not yet been accomplished even in India. We should have little exact information on Vaiṣṇavite ritual without the *Haribhaktivilāsa*, a sixteenth-century Caitanyan manual; we should know little of religious feeling without certain Bengali and Marathi poems, many of them of recent date. Our best guide to the understanding of ancient mystical movements is the attitude of Rāmakṛṣṇa in the nineteenth century. In Indian studies ancient and modern evidence alike must be taken into account; the testimony of folk-lore and that of the most erudite *kāvyas* must both make their contribution. They are all documents to be considered; and the most subtle writings are none the less authentic evidence.

Literary evidence is not, however, a faithful mirror of religious life. It emphasizes certain aspects and leaves others out of account. The extent of the treatises on Buddhism and Jainism is disproportionately large in relation to the real importance of these movements. We should know little of the position of women in India if we had nothing but the idealized representations of Sītā, Draupadī and Sāvitrī. The idealization of woman is as great as her social and religious status was low.

How, then, are we to approach Hinduism? In nearly every religion there are two levels, that of popular belief, and that of elaborated technique and speculation. In Hinduism the distinction is very deep; yet at the same time all stages of transition and coexistence are observable in it. Its elementary level is as primitive as it is possible for a religion to be, characterized by widespread idolatry (the term should not be shirked), fetishism and animism. It has been found that 80 per cent of the religious believers in Southern India are devotees of the *grāmadevatās*; and that a great number of people are Hindus in name only, and cannot even tell the Census agents whether they are Vaiṣṇavites or Śaivites. The higher levels are often very advanced. But it is significant that the elementary beliefs are constantly being endowed with new meanings. Malignant and gruesome rites and narrowly materialistic conceptions may be transformed into symbols. Veneration of the cow, that rudimentary cult which is distinctive of Hinduism, may take on a transcendent ethical value in the eyes of a Gāndhi. The myths, however worthless they may be, are not excluded from any plane of thought. No philosopher attacks orthodox mythology, as did Plato; much less the common beliefs, as did Socrates. The *Advaita* distinguishes between a lower mode of knowledge and a higher, transcendent form; and there is a parallel distinction to be observed in all religious manifestations, in the realm of speculation such as that concerning *pravṛtti* and *nivṛtti*, and in the division of society into ways of life or *āśramas*, which represents the contrast between the active life of the student or householder, and the contemplative life of the monk or the ascetic. Other religions select and eliminate; Hinduism incorporates. Its every feature assumes a distinctive importance when studied by itself. It has been said that Indian religion is essentially ritualistic; it has also been said that Indian religion dispenses with ritual. India is sometimes said to be completely Tantric, and sometimes to be given over to *bhakti*. There is an element of truth in all these contradictory statements: everything depends on what aspect is selected for consideration and from what standpoint it is regarded.

From Iran, there were probably Mazdean infiltrations in Christian times, confined to a limited area. They have left traces in the *Mithra* or *Mihira* of the *Kuṣāṇa* coins, in the *magas* or priests described in some of the *Purāṇas*, in the *Sūrya* of the *Bṛhatsaṃhitā*, who is dressed in Iranian costume, and in a few other facts of a similar kind. But the influence goes no deeper than this, and we cannot subscribe to Przyluski's belief that the *guṇa* system, which is clearly connected with the cosmic tripartition of the Veda, was inspired by Iranian models.

Very little is known about the influence of Islām on Hinduism, and the subject deserves close study. In the course of a few centuries, a quarter of the Hindu population abandoned the ancestral religion, either because they were compelled to do so by force or because they were attracted by the hope of material gains; such an event cannot be without effects. There are, in fact, traces of a few mixed sects, which we shall discuss later. But Indian literature shows hardly any Moslem influence, except, of course, the Urdū. A sixteenth-century Hindī poem, *Padmavatī*, is sometimes quoted as an example; while its subject matter and style are essentially Indian, it is *Sūfī* in spirit; but it was written by a Moslem. It seems, in fact, that in spite of undeniable resemblances, the mystical movements developed independently. If Islām did influence Hinduism, it was by provoking a counter-reaction which took the form either of an increased adherence to the sects or of a stricter enforcing of the requirements of the Hindu cult. It is hardly likely that it needed Islāmic propaganda to induce the various sects to abandon images, when the whole of Hindu teaching, from time immemorial, has emphasized the value of abstract truth and of worshipping the intangible.

As regards the influence of China, if the admittedly striking parallelism between the techniques of *Yoga* and those of Taoism lead us to assume that one borrowed from the other it would seem that the initiative must be attributed to India: for it is in India that the tradition is most firmly established. If certain texts call Tantrism the 'Chinese practice', *Cīnācāra*, the term refers to Tibet as the region from which *Vajrayāna* was diffused; it does not imply that so profoundly Indian a movement had its roots outside.

In short, India has contributed much more to religion than she has received from others. The expansion of Hinduism from at least the second century onwards over the whole of South-East Asia, from Burma to Java and Bali, is well known. The facts have been partially obscured by the predominance of Buddhism, which was usually earlier in the field than Hinduism and appeared again after it; for it never lost its hold over the masses, whereas Vaiṣṇavism and especially Śaivism tended rather to be the religions of the élite or of the State. Buddhism, free of ritual and legal requirements, was a religion more readily accepted in other countries than Hinduism, even a Hinduism which had put aside the laws of caste. But Hindu patterns have profoundly influenced iconography, the ceremonies of kingship and the very conception of what a king should be. Hindu imagery reached Tibet and the Far East through the medium of Buddhism. It should be remembered that Buddhism played little part in developing science and technology: for the diffusion of grammar or poetics, for example, it made use of treatises of Hindu inspiration, thinly disguised as Buddhist works.

The diffusion of Vaiṣṇavite and Śaivite ideas outside India is enough to show that Hinduism, too, was a missionary religion; at a very early date a Hinduist movement took root in the Hellenistic world and penetrated as far as Egypt. The decline of Hinduism after the Moslem period must not be allowed to obscure this fact. The old lawgivers say that to be a Hindu, or, more exactly, to belong to one of the three Āryan classes, means to have been born in a certain area of Hindustan, the *Āryāvarta* (or homeland of the Āryas); but this assertion need not be taken literally. Hinduism long ago advanced beyond the limits assigned to it by the laws of Manu, by means of conquest or peaceful absorption, by marriage, and by adoption. Hinduism has no word to express the process of conversion so frequently referred to in Buddhist and Jaina apologetics, books written by the converted for those to be converted; but passages can be cited from the *Mahābhārata* which show that people of low caste, enemies and foreigners were received into the Hindu fold. Many people wanted to raise their status and be admitted to *Ārya* society; others fell away from it through marriage outside its ranks and by transgressions and misfortunes. A passage of Patañjali attests that the Śakas and the Yavanas could perform sacrifices and accept food from an Ārya without contaminating it. The fact is that Hinduism is a way of life, a mode of thought, that becomes second nature. It is not so much its practices that are important, for they can be dispensed with; nor is it the Church, since it has no priesthood, or at least no sacerdotal hierarchy. The important thing is to accept certain fundamental conceptions, to acknowledge a certain 'spirituality', a term much abused in current parlance. For many Hindus it would be quite legitimate to take Jesus as *iṣṭadevatā*, without even regarding Him as an *avatāra*, so long as Indian tradition were acknowledged.

If we had a better knowledge of the social system in which this religion arose, we could more easily decide which features of it were public, and which were secret and even esoteric. We tend to regard the various *mārgas*, *yogas* and *darśanas* as absolute truths in themselves, whereas they are really aspects of the truth which exist side by side and are not mutually exclusive. On the mythological plane, the inconsistencies we sometimes discern are really non-existent. Despite the aggressive spirit of certain texts, indifference to the identity of the gods is the dominating tendency: 'May Hari hear our prayer (says the Haristuti), Hari who rules the three worlds, and whom the Śaivites worship as Śiva, the *Vedāntins* as Brahman, the Buddhists as Buddha, the *Naiyāyikas* as the Supreme Power, the Jainas as the Liberated, the *Mīmāṃsakas* as *karman*.' Even the heresies are shown to pay homage to Hari. A much-quoted passage from the *Ṛgveda* says: *Ekaṃ sad viprā bahudhā vadanti*, 'That supreme being (neuter) that is one, the holy poets say to be many'. The same sentence is found in the popular songs of the South. Hence the idea of *māyā*, the principle of change, and of *līlā*, the divine 'play' described in mythology, by which Indian thought disguises the mutual irreducibility of the One and the Many. In religion, few ideas are found to be finally irreconcilable.

The view that the outward ceremonial is intended for

the masses is in accordance with this line of thought. It is worship of the mind which is important: meditation, whether or not induced by external forms, by concrete symbol or by mental image; and mental representation, it is said, gives rise to experiences which are more concrete and more dynamic than those evoked by representations in wood and stone. Thus Hinduism prescribes a worship of the absent, just as Vedism set up a hierarchy of formulae, according to whether they were said aloud, whispered or silently thought, just as the power of silence was reverenced in ancient ritual, and as the *Brāhmaṇas* prescribed as a parallel to the Fire Oblation a *Prāṇāgnihotra* which was to take place within the worshipper himself. The absent is itself conceived in figurative terms: the imaginary pillar of the *Atharvaveda* supports the firmament; the absent *liṅga* of Chidambaram is alleged to be the most efficacious; the Ganges is present in any stretch of water correctly invoked.

Religious speculation itself moves on two levels. Each *darśana*, that is, each approach (for it would be wrong to see them as so many systems), culminates in a way of Liberation, or, as we should say, of salvation. This kind of speculation, directed primarily or ultimately towards soteriology, is in no way confined to professional philosophers. Each *Purāṇa* examines the problems of *brahman* and *prakṛti* for itself, as if it were the first to deal with the subject. Expositions of fundamental principles are found in the *Smṛti*. The *Pañcadaśī* popularizes abstruse metaphysics in an agreeable verse-form. Johnston has shown that the *Sāṃkhya* of the Epic and the *Purāṇas* is not altogether the same as the *Sāṃkhya* of the philosophers.[1]

Here we see yet another level, which resulted in a fusion of doctrines, the *Sāṃkhya-Vedānta* compromise of many ancient texts; such fusions are found at all periods: at the

[1] E. H. Johnston, *Early Sāṃkhya, an Essay on its Historical Development according to the Texts* (London, 1937).

present day we speak of the *Yoga-Vedānta*, and at one time teachers composed primers of *Nyāya-Vaiśeṣika*.

Hinduism has passed through many periods of time in which adherence to various forms of practice ebbed and flowed. In a given area, a period of idolatry would be followed by a cult which repudiated images; and a whole district would suddenly be converted to *bhakti*, or 'loving devotion', against which the old non-dualist instinct would subsequently revolt.

The part played by outside influences must be assessed when considering facts of this kind. Leaving aside the fundamental Asiatic element, the incalculable prehistoric influences, we look first to Buddhism as a possible source of influence. But in fact Buddhism does not seem to have had any positive effect on Hinduism in early times. We may suspect that the spread of Buddhism at first brought about a crystallization of the spiritual values of Hinduism, and later a relaxation of social and ritual intolerance; but nothing can be proved. All the features common to ancient Hinduism and the Pāli Canon spring from the Indian background that they both share. Very much later, in the field of philosophical speculation, we see in the *Vedānta*, in Gauḍapāda and Śaṅkara, a tendency to remould the old realism under the impetus of the idealist schools of Buddhism; and in fact Śaṅkara brahmanizes the *Great Vehicle*, as many orthodox Hindus will agree. In Kumārila and the Logicians of the seventh and ninth centuries, there arises a passionate controversy with the Buddhists, in which neither side retreats at all from its position. There is no question of influence. As for current religious practice, it is difficult to see what impact Buddhism has made on it. The foundation of monasticism in India by the Buddhists and Jainas produced no answering movement outside their own ranks until much later; and when it did come, it was in circumstances that do not suggest any direct borrowing.

It has been suggested that Indian religious iconography was inspired by that of Ancient Greece; but the material for an iconography is already to be found in the Veda, even to the description of many-armed divinities. It is hardly likely that India had to await Greek impulsion to transpose these indications into plastic form.

As we read India's literature and look at her works of art, we are impressed by her fertility in creating divinities. If, as Bergson said, 'le monde est une machine à faire des dieux', then India has contributed more than her share. Her mythology is almost as voluminous as at the Vedic period; it has the same abundance of hymnology; but its orientation is quite different. There is no longer any perceptible connection (if there ever was one) between ritual and legend. The Tantric form, a kind of dialogue between Śiva and the Goddess, is only a traditional framework. Of course there is a basic correspondence between the form of worship and the chosen divinity, and one's attitude to the divinity; the details of the plastic representation are meaningful, the arrangement of the hair, the dress, the ornaments, the facial expression and the gestures of hand and finger, the *mudrās*, which have a language of their own. But these are primarily static representations: ritual draws its inspiration from a divine posture or *āsana*; it does not attempt to reproduce a story. Already in the Veda, however, one can see a tendency for ritual to become a dramatic scenario, giving the impression of a myth in action. In the *Indramahotsava*, the festival of Indra's standard, the king has a tree felled, sets up the trunk in the middle of the city with banners bearing pictures of Indra, and makes offerings to it; finally it is rolled into the river to drift with the stream. This ceremony is thought to be associated with a story going back to the days of battles between gods and demons, as in the *Brāhmaṇas*: the story went that the gods borrowed Indra's standard in order to overcome their enemies. The *dīpālī*, a lamp-lighting festival still widely observed today, though in a far less colourful form than formerly, was originally a carnival representing the one-day reign upon earth of the demon Bali, who, when vanquished by Indra, was granted the privilege of returning to the earth once a year to exercise his old power. The link between ritual and image is very different from the primitive one, or rather there is no longer any ritual, by which I mean liturgy in the strict sense of the term. The public ceremonies of Vedic times were not imitated even in the most spectacular festivals of classical India; and private cult-practice contains no mythiform elements. At the most there is an occasional symbolic transposition, like the 'purification of the elements', which reflects the theme of *kuṇḍalinī*. The officiant's aim is to make the five elements, of which his body is composed, merge into one another by means of formulae and controlled breathing, until, little by little, consciousness itself dissolves into the original *prakṛti*. The rite of the ascent of the *kuṇḍalinī* is based on a more impressive piece of imagery: that of the coiled serpent that sleeps within the body and can be aroused by a certain technique, to penetrate one after the other the six superimposed circles until it reaches the 'opening of Brahman' on the top of the head and brings about the union of the being with Śiva. But there is no supporting myth underlying the imagery of this technique. Moreover, when the mind by meditation evolves the figure of a god, as in the case of Gaṇeśa, his characteristics really represent memories of certain symbols translated into actions.

Let us consider the divinities again. Henceforward they are quite distinct from natural phenomena, without, however, being any the less complex. Solar myth, for instance, was relegated to the background, though it was later to enjoy a brief revival under Iranian influence. Grierson put forward the view that Viṣṇu, the sun-god of the Veda, represents a continuance of the solar theme;[1] but the theory is not convincing. It is true that there are Hindu myths about the origin of the world which, if they do not deal with the first beginnings, at least describe the later stages of creation: the descent of the Ganges, the establishment of the cosmic *liṅga*, and the churning of the waters. But after all, no mythology can ignore the act of creation. These are not, moreover, the dominant themes of Hindu mythology. Fertility myths are perhaps more prominent in it, though J. J. Meyer has placed rather too much emphasis on them;[2] too many disparate elements tend to be grouped together under this convenient heading. But the theme is certainly present, often appearing in the form of sexual exploits. That teeming sexuality, which is already traceable in the Veda, now appears in many of the gods. It is the price paid for the asceticism and emasculation imposed on India. In Śiva it takes on a mystical aspect; in Kāma it is predominantly literary; in Gaṇeśa it is popular in expression (though at the same time mystical); in Pradyumna and Kṛṣṇa it is idyllic, in Skanda and the southern Subrahmaṇya aggressive and indecent; in Indra several aspects are combined. The typically Hindu figure of Gaṇeśa admits of various interpretations, according to the level on which one sees him (for in the gods, too, there are different levels of significance, ranging from the literal to the transcendent plane): this ancient elephant-genie of the jungle, as M. Foucher calls him,[3] when seen in his popular aspect, is a libidinous figure who was to be used in the symbolism of Tantrism. The eroticism which is sometimes considered to be characteristic of Hinduism, and

[1] 'The Monotheistic Religion of Ancient India', *Asiatic Quart. Rev.*, 28 (1909), p. 115.

[2] *Trilogie altindischer Mächte und Feste der Vegetation* (Zürich und Leipzig, 1937).

[3] In his preface to A. Getty's book, *Gaṇeśa, a Monograph on the Elephant-Faced God* (Oxford, 1936).

which appears most fully in the Tantric cult, and in the extreme forms of *bhakti*, is already present in myth.

Battle-myths are frequent and are usually associated with myths of the type just described. The struggles of Śiva against Arjuna and Śiśupāla, his attack on Dakṣa and his sacrifice, probably reflect the opposition that the Śiva cult met with before it was finally established. Myths of expansion, like those of Rāma and Agastya, are probably based on memories of former conquests. The twofold aspect of destroyer and protector, under which both the Goddess and Śiva appear, is the working of the Vedic legacy of ambivalence; or rather, the actions of the gods are thought of as encompassing many aspects of alternating activity and rest. An interesting example is the battle cycle of the Goddess, her fights with demons as in the Veda: it is Caṇḍī who destroys the Asuras and their chief Mahiṣa, who had in vain disguised himself as a buffalo. Or again, the Goddess, having told the demon Śumbha who desired her that no one could win her except by overcoming her in battle (a well-known motif in legends of warrior-virgins), routs the armies sent against her one after the other. But there are other, very different portrayals, such as that of the Satī who throws herself into the flames because of the quarrel between Dakṣa, her father, and Śiva, her husband (a story that explains the origin of the practice known as *satī*); commemoration of the spot where her bones fell to the ground was the origin of setting up *pīṭhas* (sacred places). Pārvatī takes a vow of asceticism in order to tempt Śiva; thus mythology illustrates that great driving-force of religious life, the asceticism which subdues the passions. There is the food-giving Goddess of Bengali legend, the Serpent-Goddess Mānasā, the ogress Kālī, who demands human sacrifice; there are the ogresses or lesser spirits, Śītalā or Smallpox, Ṣaṣṭhī who watches over the sixth day of the new-born child's life; and lastly the divine Mother, the supreme *śakti*, the energy of the gods. This was one of the abstract forces of the Veda, now envisaged as an immensely powerful woman. The patriotic exalting of India as the mother-country that has arisen in recent times has helped to keep this image alive. Even the male gods have been drawn into this intensive feminization of mythical conceptions. Tukārām calls upon Viṭṭhala, that is, Viṣṇu, as his mother. The *grāmadevatās* are female. Another dominant conception is that of the child-god, unknown in the Veda, such as Kṛṣṇa and Kumāra (especially as he appears in the South, under the name of Subrahmaṇya).

The attributes of the gods share in the process of deification: their animal mounts, their jewels, their weapons or implements, the images associated with them. The worship of particular aspects of the gods becomes predominant, a tendency already discernible in the invocations of the *Yajurveda* to Agni Gṛhapati, Agni Sviṣṭakṛt, Agni Vaiśvānara, and so on. There are twenty-four *niṣṭhās* or aspects of Viṣṇu, such as the bird Garuḍa, the *liṅga*, and the disc Sudarśana, each one having a symbolic meaning. The function of iconography is to give concrete shape to some of these conceptions, which might otherwise have been indefinite in outline.

The legends of the gods seldom give us a consistent biography of them. The two life-stories that do exist both relate to deified heroes. Rāma is the type of the victorious prince, whose name is probably linked with the memory of the Aryan invasion of Southern India and Ceylon. His elevation to divine status was brought about by gradual stages; Rāmaist sects are late in appearing, although it is alleged that there is mention of a god Rāma in a passage of Vālmīki (which may be an interpolation).

Kṛṣṇa's deification took place much more speedily: we can see it happening in the theophany of the *Gītā*, and it is at least possible that it provided the inspiration for Rāma-worship. That Kṛṣṇa was originally a mortal is very probable: he was a tribal chief, brought up in concealment by shepherds so that he should be kept safe from his uncle, the cruel king Kaṃsa; this is of course a folk-lore theme, but it is not far removed from the events of everyday life. Kṛṣṇa founds cities, and settles near the mouths of the Indus. In the war with the Pāṇḍavas, he sides with the five brothers who turn out to be his cousins: he now shows himself to be a cunning and unscrupulous counsellor, but his advice brings about their victory. His last days are dark and terrible, like the endings of so many heroes: he is fated to bring about the destruction of his people and to look on unmoved. Another strand is interwoven with this warrior-cycle, that of the youthful Kṛṣṇa, a pastoral demi-god who sings and dances with the shepherdesses. Most of the Indian themes, apart from that of asceticism, are found in this complex legend, which alone provides a consistent narrative of the hero's '*enfances*', like the mediaeval *chansons de geste*. It was later to be imitated in the *Adhyātmarāmāyaṇa*, which substitutes Rāma as the hero. The conception of the divine shepherd has been an important one in the history of erotic mysticism.

There are no such complete mythical cycles associated with the great gods. The conception of the *Trimūrti*, whose aspects are Brahman the creator, Viṣṇu the preserver and Śiva the destroyer, is in accordance with ancient thought, but it makes only a late appearance in the texts and never gained much credence. While Brahman remains a somewhat insubstantial figure (though for some reason he plays a part in the Buddhism of the Pāli Canon), a great accretion of later detail was built round the other two. Viṣṇu absorbed local divinities into himself, such as the Viṭhobā of the Marathi country, and Veṅkateśa and Tirupati in the South. Nārāyaṇa, who was probably a water-god, was identified with him.

In comparison with Kṛṣṇa or the Goddess, Viṣṇu and Śiva seem to be *dei otiosi*; they have some of the characteristics of the ancient Prajāpati. Sylvain Lévi declared that they were '*raisons sociales*'.[1] Śiva enters upon a long period of inactivity as a *Yogin*; in Tantric representations he appears as a white and lifeless form at the side of a gigantic *Devī*. The *Śatapatha* reminds us that originally he had not even a name (VI, 1, 3, 8). When he wants to take action, he does so by proxy. In Bengal there is even a domestic Śiva, a kind of householder with a wife and sons. True, there is also Śiva the dancer, whose movements bring the cosmic forces into being; but this is really a piece of animated symbolism rather than an action performed by him. Viṣṇu, too, very frequently appears as a reclining god, vessel of the magical sleep in which the world is 'thought'. He sends forth the *vyūhas*, emanations of power which are diffused through the cosmos, and by whose agency he can be present in the categories which create the forms. These *vyūhas* are an artifice of the theologians, intended as a demonstration of Viṣṇu's part in the three fundamental functions performed by the *Trimūrti*.

The theory of the *avatāras* or incarnations of Viṣṇu has a wider appeal. This is a conception fundamental to mythology, and, I would almost say, to the Indian mentality. India's great men have so frequently in the past been regarded as *avatāras* of the deity, and the tendency can still occasionally be perceived today. It is the equivalent of our doctrine of 'the Word made flesh'; and, as Barth said, it is the means by which striving after a higher monotheism can be reconciled with the irradicable tendency to worship multiple forms.[2] In other words, the object was to safe-

[1] *L'Inde et le Monde* (Paris, 1926), p. 83.

[2] A. Barth, *Les religions de l'Inde* (Paris, 1882; new edition in the *Works* of Barth, vol. 1, 1914, p. 153. English translation: *The Religions of India*, London, 1882).

guard monism while at the same time acknowledging the plurality of divine manifestations and the very principle of divine intervention in the human sphere, or providence. But this providence is not concerned with individual man, but with humanity as a whole: its workings were accomplished in the remote past, and have little to do with present-day humanity, which is perhaps unworthy of salvation. The acknowledged purpose of the *avatāras* is to save *dharma* when it is imperilled, the gods, the Brahmans and the devout. The clearest formulation of this is found in the *Gītā*: 'Whenever the Law falters and chaos threatens, I send forth my Self. I am born in succeeding ages to protect the good and destroy the evil.'

The *avatāras* were originally independent legends which came to centre on Viṣṇu, perhaps because from the beginning Viṣṇu was the symbol of the propagation of the divine: they are legends of prowess over demons, of the usual type, which portray a hero, or a creature gifted with superhuman powers, in animal or semi-animal form. The last *avatār* is still to come: the White Horse which is to be its form is the symbol of a kind of Messiah, analogous to the figure who in Buddhism is called *Maitreya*, and who has other names in Iran.

Every Vaiṣṇavite system has its own interpretation of the *avatāras*. A distinction has arisen between partial *avatāras*, both primary and secondary, which represent only part of the Supreme Being, and complete *avatāras*, among which Rāma and Kṛṣṇa are often included. Eventually the theory began to encroach upon Śaivism. Viṣṇu no longer provided sufficient material for it, but his attributes played their part in the larger picture.

This, then, is the Hindu conception of the world of the gods; an overcrowded world, prolific of all kinds of personifications, some destined to live on, others only adventitious. There are very few elements capable of carrying religious significance that escape divinization. The few non-individuated groups of the Veda, like the Maruts and Rudras, have given rise to many kinds of demons, who intervene in human affairs on occasion, *Yakṣas*, *Vidyādharas*, *Nāgas* and many more. There is little sign of a hierarchical order among all these beings, but their attributes are usually very well-defined, as in the case of the *Lokapālas* who are connected with a cult of the cardinal points. For a more highly-developed systematization, we have to look outside Hinduism altogether, to the cosmological scholasticism of the Jainas and the 'pure regions' of the *Great Vehicle*.

There is no demoniac figure of any importance in Hinduism, any more than there is in Vedism. It offers nothing comparable to Māra, whose name the Hindu poets disguise by making it a synonym of the God of Love. Demons have a tendency to appear as devotees, like Rāvaṇa, the enemy of Rāma, and Vṛtra, the dragon killed by Indra. Tulsīdās says that Rāma was incarnated to rescue Rāvaṇa from an undeserved fate. The new mythologists were probably deterred from creating fresh figures of the infernal world by the ambivalence that still persisted in the sphere of divine significances.

IV

Hinduism: II

We know much more about the behaviour of the gods than about what they meant to man. Each text has its own attitude in this matter, the fact being that the gods are really superfluous in Indian religion, and the essentials could have been covered by the theory of *karman* and its consequences, by the quest for Liberation. Yet the gods are included in all doctrinal systems; not even the 'atheist' schools deny the existence of divine beings. But many texts portray them as beings of a limited power. They are gods who have been 'brought forth' or who have 'come into existence' as in the *Sāṃkhya*; they are not only powerless to intervene between man and *karman*, they are themselves subject to this law. This is a position not unlike that of the Buddhist '*devas*'. According to the *Śaivasiddhānta*, they cannot attain Liberation. They are aids to prayer and meditation, rather like our saints.

The supreme deity is on quite a different plane, whether he is known as Viṣṇu—which may also mean Rāma or Kṛṣṇa—or as Śiva. The Supreme Being is no longer above the world of myth, as in the Veda; he now plays a part in mythology, though on an exalted level. This may perhaps suggest that we are approaching a conception of God rather than gods; and when we find that from the *Śvetāśvatara-Upaniṣad* onwards, the Īśvara or Bhagavant is spoken of as a being demonstrably beyond all contingency and variation, this impression is strengthened. But it is a complex question. In Śaṅkara the idea of God belongs now to the sphere of higher knowledge, now to that of lower knowledge, according to whether or not it is conceived of as without qualities; in other words, whether or not it is the repository of the impersonal neuter force called *brahman*. It is admissible only by those who have not attained the highest stage of perfection. Similarly *ātman* varies between the old, semi-abstract idea of the Upaniṣadic *ātman*, and the new, concrete idea of *jīva*. The idea of the neuter *brahman*, which had been threatened by that of Īśvara from the middle Upaniṣadic period onwards, was re-established as a principle of speculative thought by Śaṅkara: *brahman* alone is the Absolute, the Transcendent, but it is an impersonal, neuter principle; Īśvara is its restatement in terms of person, but it is an imperfect restatement. To the Indian mind, God is 'l'hypostase déficiente de l'Absolu', as M. Lacombe has said.[1] The world is usually envisaged as an attribute of the divine. In short, the divine is both transcendent and immanent; traces of the original pantheism are still apparent. There are, of course, endless gradations of thought, but on the whole we may say that the negative definition of the *Bṛhadāraṇyaka-Upaniṣad* gains the widest acceptance. From early times it was said that the Supreme Being is silence.

Let us look at the *Arthapañcaka*, a thirteenth-century South Indian text by Loka Piḷḷai. The Īśvara here is fivefold; he is a personal god in the form of Viṣṇu, dwelling in the paradise Vaikuṇṭha; his being is 'diffused' among many forms (in accordance with the conception of the *vyūhas*) and he performs the trinity of cosmic functions; he is a being capable of assuming special forms to appear on earth (the conception of the *avatāras*); he is the inward guiding power, *antaryāmin*, the equivalent of *ātman*; and finally he is the *arcā*, the holy image made for cult-worship.

[1] (Orally). Cf. Olivier Lacombe, *L'Absolu selon le Vedānta* (Paris, 1937).

Of course, the poets of the people and the crowd-preachers have simpler conceptions. A Southern poet, probably of the eighth century, says: 'I look for bliss neither to Indra, nor to Viṣṇu, nor to Brahman; for me only one god exists, Thou, our Supreme Being.' Rāmakṛṣṇa in the nineteenth century approaches the idea of the Christian God; but he, like many others, has a strange mixture of beliefs: in moments of ecstasy he worships the *brahman* without qualities; in ordinary devotion he includes Kṛṣṇa or Rāma, and Śiva or the Goddess in his worship.

The relationship between God and Man is, in large measure, lacking: there is no reciprocity. God is not a familiar despot like Jahveh; there is nothing of that somewhat cynical bargaining spirit towards him which we sense when a poet of the Veda says, 'Do thou give if thou wishest me to give'. We have seen that the idea of Providence was late in appearing, and did not impose itself strongly when it did appear; the idea of a God who had pity on human suffering made even slower progress. Grierson remarks that it was Tulsīdās in the seventeenth century who initiated the theme of divine compassion;[1] yet it is foreshadowed three millennia earlier, in the hymns to Varuṇa.

The transition from the neuter to the personal principle, and the increasing predominance of representations in personal form, were brought about by the operation of a new factor of great importance, known as *bhakti*. The term itself is old, but the propagation of the idea it represents is relatively recent, though we cannot say how or where it took place. We should be cautious of attaching undue importance to the prosopopoeia of the *Bhāgavatapurāṇa*, in which *Bhakti* personified is made to say, 'I was born in the Dravidian country'. As affective 'participation' of the soul in the divine, *bhakti* presupposes an object distinct from the

[1] 'Tulasī Dāsa, Poet and Religious Reformer', *J. R. Asiat. Soc.*, 1903, p. 447.

subject. It would not therefore gain currency in a purely monistic environment; it was better adjusted to the atheist *Sāṃkhya* than the *Advaita Vedānta*, for the *Sāṃkhya* was pluralist and relatively realist. Hence *bhakti* first emerges in the *Upaniṣads* of *Sāṃkhya* inspiration, especially in the *Śvetāśvatara* which Schrader called 'the gateway to Hinduism'.[1] It was developed in the *Bhagavadgītā*, in which the *Sāṃkhya-Yoga* concepts also dominate the speculative plane, and much later in the *Bhāgavatapurāṇa* which is as much *Sāṃkhya* as *Vedāntin*. *Bhakti* has always been better adapted to a Vaiṣṇavite background, probably because the emotive imagery of Rāma and Kṛṣṇa was more fitted to sustain its conceptions than the rather more abstract forms of doctrinal Śaivism. But it was an obscure impulse of the masses that brought it into prominence, an impulse that probably originated in that centre of mystical outpourings which produced the literature of the Southern 'saints'; this would indicate the seventh century as the approximate date for the renaissance of *bhakti*. The Islamic hypothesis is unnecessary. In brief the theory is that a God without attributes is inaccessible, and that there must be an intercessor. In the absence of a founder or prophet, God 'incarnate' must be at once the intermediary and the prophet of *bhakti*.

This religious conception was soon claimed or reclaimed by speculative thought. Those powerful movements of which Rāmānuja is the highest expression, freed themselves from the impersonal *brahman* and adopted *bhakti*. Rāmānuja defines it as 'an enduring recollection, having the nature of an intuitive perception, which takes the form of abounding love for the object of recollection, the supreme Self'. Elsewhere he calls it a calm, continuous movement, 'like a stream of flowing oil'. Others say that it is a *sevā*, the attitude of a devoted servant to his master. Gradually the word acquires many shades of associated meaning. Vallabha

[1] F. Otto Schrader, *Der Hinduismus* (Tübingen, 1930), p. 1.

develops the idea of *prapatti*, an 'abandonment' of the being to the divine; the initiative is then God's, and he dispenses his grace; *prasāda*, and *puṣṭi* or 'efflorescence', are the terms designating this new aspect of belief. Theologians argue whether man receives grace without any action of his own, as a kitten is caught up by the scruff of its neck and dragged away from danger by the mother-cat, or whether, like a monkey that clings to its mother, he must make a personal effort—a less Jansenist theory. In theological terms this dispute is but another aspect of the old conflict between *daiva* or fatality and *puruṣakāra* or the value of human actions, between *pravṛtti*, the doctrine of action, and *nivṛtti*, the doctrine of abstention.

The theory becomes increasingly subtle with the passage of time. Formerly the easy path, the path of simple love, it later tends to become the hard path to many people. Already in the *Bhāgavatapurāṇa* nine degrees of *bhakti* are distinguished: further subdivisions are recognized in the Vaiṣṇavite scholasticism of the Caitanya school. In India to penetrate a subject more deeply is to classify it further. The evolution of the word *bhakti* is comparable to that of the Latin *pietas*. *Bhakti* originally meant participation in a rite, just as *pietas* was the meticulous discharge of one's duty to the gods; *piaculum* was the practice of religion understood as the payment of a debt. Gradually the Sanskrit term came to mean (as in Tulsīdās) religion as a whole. When the word has reached this stage of meaning, then it is true to say that the whole of India is steeped in *bhakti*.

This has unexpected consequences. Rāmaite *bhakti* remains relatively pure; it is the *bhakti* of a wife. Kṛṣṇaite *bhakti* is erotic; it is the *bhakti* of a concubine; religious beatitude comes to be conceived as a sort of carnal intercourse with the god in the idyllic setting of *Vṛndāvana*. I cannot say whether religious feeling profited greatly by this development, but it was an undoubted gain for literature. *Bhakti* gave fresh impetus to religious inspiration; it created a mixed genre, of which the *Gītagovinda* (a pastoral poem that reminds us of the Song of Songs) was the prototype. The stimulus of an emotion, it is thought, arouses religious feeling; generally, of course, it is the stimulus of love, but it may also be that of hatred. Tulsīdās says that God's anger is as precious as his love; and we are told that Prince Śiśupāla gained Liberation because of his hatred for Kṛṣṇa. The mediaeval troubadours portrayed love as a legal code, and drew up a set of rules for it; similarly, Vaiṣṇavite theologians conceive of *bhakti* in terms of rhetoric. *Rasas* and *bhāvas*, moods and emotional states repeatedly described by writers on poetics and the drama, are given mystical significance. The final end is the highest *rasa*, *ujjvala*, which represents the Eros of the god Kṛṣṇa. For the *Sahajiyās* worship remains platonic; it is directed towards a woman deemed to be unattainable, for example a chaste married woman.

Cosmogonic speculation, on both space and time, has gained greatly in profundity since the Veda. In the realm of space, we find extremely elaborate conceptions, such as the cosmic Egg or *brahmāṇḍa*, together with the various celestial, earthly and subterranean spheres of which it is composed. The Earth is in the central position: its pivotal point is Mount Meru, above which stands the pole star. Around Mount Meru lie the four island-continents, like the four quarters of a circle, situated one at each cardinal point. The early Buddhist conception is very similar. From the *Purāṇas* onwards it is replaced by a portrayal of concentric islands and seas, surrounding the principal continent, *Jambudvīpa*. This is a tangible representation of the world. As an explanation of first principles, the theory is sometimes advanced that there existed a material substratum or continuum, the *prakṛti*, containing the quality-substances called *guṇas*, a term which makes its appearance in a passage of mystical symbolism in the *Atharva*. The *guṇas*, by mingling together, create the material elements that make up the world: this is a rudimentary atomism, which formed the basis of the evolutive conception of the cosmos put forward in *Sāṃkhya* doctrine.

Indian speculation on time expanded the age of the world to infinity; it conceived a series of *kalpas*, eras of creation, each *kalpa* consisting of a thousand great ages or *mahāyugas*, and each *mahāyuga* consisting of four *yugas*. M. Filliozat has shown that there is agreement between some of the Indian calculations and the figures arrived at by Berosus and Heraclitus for the 'great years'.[1] The basis of the computation is an astronomical fact, as Biot perceived.[2] The 'great year' of 4,320,000 years is only an expansion of the Vedic *yuga* of five years, which was the time taken by the sun and moon to accomplish a certain number of complete revolutions simultaneously; 4,320,000 years is the period taken by the planets to accomplish the same number of revolutions.

The present era, like every era, is made up of four periods; we are now in the bad period or *kaliyuga*, which began at a date corresponding to about 3000 B.C. This period of retrogression and pessimism represents the aftermath following on the ideal of the Golden Age, an ideal held in common by most ancient civilizations. The difficulties and dangers prevailing at the time when the system seems to have been laid down helped to gain credence for it: it provided justification for inveighing against the morals of the age and for denouncing those who are 'swans outside and crows within', as Tulsīdās was to say later.

[1] Communication to the Société Asiatique de Paris, 9th April, 1948; cf. *J. Asiat.*, 1948–49 (Annuaire), p. 80, and 1950, p. 374.

[2] J. B. Biot, *Études sur l'astronomie indienne et sur l'astronomie chinoise* (Paris, 1862), p. 37.

The *Purāṇas* were written in a spirit of 'denial of history' and 'fear of history', as M. Éliade says.[1] But there is a sort of pre-scientific intuition at the root of this theory of the progressive worsening of man's state; at all events the system of four ages was retained in Indian astronomical treatises, for it was considered to provide a satisfactory principle of explanation. It should be added that each *kalpa* is divided into fourteen equal cycles, called 'intervals between the Manus'. The Manus are regents of the world, combining in themselves the functions of legislator and primitive king or father of the human race.

The end of the world is usually conceived as a conflagration followed by flood: it seems possible that this conception is referred to in verses 39–40 of the Atharvan hymn that we have already noticed as mentioning the *guṇas*. The end of the world, the *pralaya*, is not final, however. There will be other worlds after it, as there were before it. All these conceptions are dependent on the primordial idea of 'perpetual recurrence'. The image often used to illustrate this idea is that of a wheel that turns but does not move forward.

On the subject of the next world, there is an intermingling of widely-differing conceptions. There are widely-accepted traditions about the *pretas*, departed spirits who have not yet attained a definite status like the *pitṛs*. There is the more highly developed idea of a judgment of the dead by Yama; and finally there is the idea of the direct ascension of the soul to heaven. Heaven and hell belong to the sphere of popular belief, but this did not deter some theologians from adopting these conceptions, nor the late *Vedānta* from reintroducing ideas of Paradise into its description of the nature of Liberation. Madhva puts forward the theory of an everlasting hell.

[1] Mircea Éliade, *Le Mythe de l'Éternel Retour* (Paris, 1949), esp. p. 207.

The theory of transmigration is reconciled, as far as possible, with all these ideas. After the death of the body, it is incumbent on the soul to assume the guardianship of another body in one of the three realms in which the living substance of the world is distributed. This is called *saṃsāra*, a word that makes a hesitant appearance in some of the old *Upaniṣads*, and means, properly, the universal circulation of all creatures. The *Gītā* calls it 'the great fear'; it is more frightening than the idea of hell, because man can see for himself its endless continuation. According to the Pythagorean theory of reincarnation, it was attained after a mystic initiation ceremony. But this is not so in Indian *saṃsāra*, which is a popular doctrine open to everyone, and is expressed in crude forms, even in such a weighty text as the *Laws of Manu*. *Saṃsāra* in India is a necessary auxiliary to the theory of *karman*. The form of the reborn body, in other words the status of the creature in its new existence, depends on *karman*. The old cosmogonic representations of superimposed heavens and hells and states of being were modified or reconstructed in accordance with this new doctrine. The universe becomes the setting and the tool of a universal moral law.

The basis of *karman* is a scientific one, if we agree that it is derived from the Vedic conception of *ṛta*: in this way, *karman* is seen to be the natural order of things rooted in the moral order and in causality. Action generates invisible energy, unique of its kind (*apūrva*), which influences the soul and regulates the destiny of the individual. The initial assumption is that actions are eternal: they follow the spirit throughout its present and future lives, identifying it unerringly 'as the calf finds its mother in a herd of many cows'. Man is born as a debt, to use the vigorous phrase of the *Śatapathabrāhmaṇa*; his existence is a 'long sequence of borrowing and paying back' (Éliade).[1] *Kar-*

[1] Op. cit., p. 145.

scribes disinterested action; desire alone corrupts. According to the *Nyāya*, discussion and debate are among the paths that lead to Liberation. Even alchemy, *rasaśāstra*, can lead to it, in that it teaches transubstantiation; Nāthism, as it is called, envisages a profound change in the body which would preserve it from all decay.

The nature of Liberation varies appreciably according to whether the divine is represented as personal or impersonal. Thus the *Advaita*, which sets up the impersonal *brahman* as the supreme principle, conceives the union of the liberated soul with the *brahman* as a dissolution of personality; it is compared to a river running into the sea. The *Yogavāsiṣṭha* says that it is like the condition of a stone. Others compare it to that mysterious state that lies beyond 'deep sleep', the 'fourth' state, as it is called through inability to define it: similarly, in Vedic times a fourth *pāda*, transcending the three visible *pādas* of the cosmos, was recognized. Yet even in the post-Śaṅkaran *Advaita*, there emerge activist conceptions of the state of the Liberated, possibly under the influence of *Mahāyāna* Buddhism.

In an atheist system like ancient *Sāṃkhya*, Liberation is a state of illumination with no object to illuminate, a mirror that reflects nothing; there is no consciousness; it is a state verging on nothingness, a condition of absolute 'isolation' (*kaivalya*). The theism of *Yoga*, on the other hand, conceives of union and integration. The philosophy of Vaiṣṇavism shows a conception which is perhaps more highly developed, according to which Liberation is union with the personal god. *Bhakti* occupies a place of special importance; far from being thought of merely as a path, however, it replaces the idea of Liberation. Various stages of union are recognized, but the personality is generally preserved, and sensual conceptions are sometimes associated with it. Other doctrines, such as the Śaivism of Kashmir, preach the complete fusion of the spirit in the Paramaśiva.

man is both the future justification of past actions and th explanation of the causes that have made our present li as it is. Its logical result would be a complete determinisı like that advocated in the early days of Buddhism by t adepts of Gośāla, the Ājīvikas. But the principle was usua modified in practice, for it tended to have an annihilati effect on normal activity. Hinduism, moreover, has s dom approached the problem systematically. The relati ship between *karman* and the divine presence in the wo its effect on character, its legal, aesthetic and physical c sequences, were all considered, besides its specifically r gious consequences. But on the other hand the difficult reconciling the theory with human liberty was ha touched upon. *Karman* helped to make the *ātman* the ject of contemplation, which had for so long been tu towards the infinite by the vistas of cosmogony.

From now on, the question of how the soul can be from the cycle of rebirth constitutes the whole of reli speculation. The principle can only be overthrown all action is spent, when the spirit is like a potter wheel is no longer driven and ceases to turn. It i enough to refrain from action, not only because man this impossible, but also because it would not anni previous *karman*. The solution lies in following out end one of the paths that lead to Liberation; amo surest is *Yoga*, a technique that aspires to confer powers. In this way the immortality of the Liber attained. *Bhakti*, if carried out with sufficient thorou is another means to the goal; so is the appercep reality, as taught by the *Vedānta*; and so is the way o which we shall discuss later. There is hardly any which, in given conditions, India does not accept a If certain texts speak of the journey as very difficult of more popular inspiration, stress the value of mor everyday principles of morality in the effort. The (

As M. de Glasenapp says, the functioning of the world then becomes a process of objectifying the god's consciousness.[1]

Other questions abound; for example whether all souls are capable of Liberation, or whether there is predestination; or whether or not Liberation can be attained durin{ man's lifetime. The various systems give different answers. Some doctrines conceive of a hitherto unknown human category, the *jīvanmukta* or 'liberated in life', whose spiritual state should be carefully observed (so far as it is possible to do so): India has surely never lacked men of this kind, from the time of the *ṛṣis* to the present day.

A great deal has been said about Indian pessimism; and its presence in *karman* and *saṃsāra* cannot be denied. The *Upaniṣads* represent the end of a period of happiness that derived from the Vedic atmosphere of well-being. The Parable at the Well in the *Mahābhārata* says that the world is a fearsome jungle. But the evil is not beyond forgiveness; there is no everlasting punishment; all suffering is justified, by Indian standards. Here at last is a religion that gives an objective account of the problem of evil. Moreover, one's state may eventually improve, and this remote consolation can itself help to free the spirit that is condemned to be reborn. Lastly, and most important, it is within every man's power to transcend the human state, if he has the courage and if a *guru* shows him the path.

The *karmamārga*, or way of ritual, has always been one of the principal paths. Although it was opposed by some systems and passed over by others, ritual remained a living force, just as much as the mythical beliefs that it distantly reflects. India without religious practice is inconceivable; in fact, the sphere of this practice was notably extended after the Vedic period.

It is true that the solemn rites of antiquity survive only

[1] H. von Glasenapp, *Die Philosophie der Inder* (Stuttgart, 1949), p. 279.

as show-pieces, scenes of simulated splendour immortalized in inscriptions. Mentions of them are found from the Śuṅgas onwards, possibly indicating a reaction against the State Buddhism instituted by Aśoka. Animal sacrifices are occasionally attested, despite the sects that urged *ahiṃsā*, but they do not seem to stem directly from the Vedic *Paśu*; they are particularly associated with the cult of Kālī, and more especially in Bengal. The function of the old *Śrauta* offices is supplied by the spectacular side of Hinduism, pilgrimages, processions, visits to the *tīrthas*, and such festivals as still contain religious elements. We know little enough of the festivals and pilgrimages of antiquity, in spite of the *māhātmyas* appended to Purāṇic literature, which are impressive rather than detailed; we should like to be able to draw up a calendar of festivals and a map of pilgrimage routes, which would tell us a great deal about the methods of transport both of men and goods. As well as the regular festivals, there were ceremonies like the *Abhiṣeka*, or royal enthronement, which is based on the old *Rājasūya*, but introduces into it new procedures reflecting the growing prestige of the regional and imperial monarchies. The voluntary self-immolation of the '*satīs*' is in part a survival of the old *puruṣamedha* or human sacrifice, and the action certainly has a religious character. In private cult-practice, the Vedic elements remained more or less unchanged, at least in the matter of the sixteen *saṃskāras*, which are accepted even by the Buddhists and Jainas. They form part of *dharma*, and enable the young Indian to enter Aryan society or guarantee him its privileges.

New forms of worship arise that stand midway between the public and private cults. Their characteristic is that they are *pūjās*, a word not yet fully explained, which indicates worship of the holy image, preferably in the temple. In principle this is an individual cult, although it is public, and it may go back to an ancient hospitality rite: it resembles the ceremonies depicting the reception of King Soma, at the beginning of the *Agniṣṭoma*. Its purpose is to prepare a reception for the divinity present in the image, who is clothed, adorned, fed and couched. Perfumes, flowers and lights, all things of which little or no mention is made in the ancient cult, now become essential to the ceremony. If the rite is to be effective, the image must have been consecrated by what is called the establishment of the breath. The setting-up of the idol constitutes a separate ceremony, a notable feature of which is the curious practice of opening its eyes.

The liturgy proper has quite fallen into desuetude. It is true that we have little detailed knowledge of Hindu cult-practice throughout the centuries, least of all of the Śaivite cult, of which no clear idea can be obtained from contemporary manuals. But whenever we can discern anything of it, there is only a very approximate correspondence with the ancient code of closely-packed injunctions and formulae, and the skilful orchestration of the old *sūtras*.

A formula is no longer linked to a definite action; it develops independently. Often it is a murmur (the usual name is *japa*, which originally referred to the recitation of certain *yajus*); its content may be a long litany, such as the 1008 names of Viṣṇu or Śiva. The *puraścaraṇa* to Brahman consists of 32,000 repetitions, according to the *Mahānirvāṇatantra*. The effectiveness of the formula or *mantra* lies not so much in the words as in the vital power with which it is invested as a result of various mechanical devices. Very often the actual acoustic qualities of the sound-units, and still more their potentialities, are of greater importance than the meaning. Words are formed arbitrarily, or alterations are made in their normal structure. Disconnected phrases are also found, as for example in the recitation of the Pāśupatas, where such phrases are accompanied by hysterical manifestations. The discomfort caused by *prāṇā-yāma* may have been the partial cause of these abnormalities, which remind us, on a larger scale, of the *stobhas* that arose in Vedic chant. The 'germ' of the *mantra* is used by itself; the concluding resonances of the sacred syllable '*oṃ*' become the subject of a whole series of speculations. Underlying all this is the idea that the recitation of the *mantra*, even when inaudible, is the essential reality. For Tulsīdās, who is quite opposed to ritualistic religion, the Name of Rāma is greater than Rāma, and the divine Name is greater than any divinity. The sacred word is an essential implement of *bhakti*: it represents the impregnation of the word by *bhakti*.

The formula was reinforced by gestures, *mudrās*, which helped to keep its form intact: the technique of the *mudrās* is still preserved even to the Far East. There are the *nyāsas*, or placing of the hands on the different parts of the body associated with various divinities. There are the diagrams or *yantras*, which express the visual element of meditation, image or formula: they are geometrical figures, composed of circles, triangles and lotus-petals, often with letters inscribed on them. The *yantra* is conceived as a miniature temple; the *Śrīyantra*, the finest of the series, has four openings, flights of steps, and a sanctuary where the chosen divinity dwells. The disposition of the triangles represents the male and female sexual organs, instruments of the *unio mystica*; and the whole is framed by a wavy line, *śiśirita*, 'trembling as if with cold'.

But the *yantra* is after all only an image, and beyond it lies the sphere of pure meditation. The Indians recognized that the mental image can be richer and fuller than any visual image, and that the reproach of idolatry could not be levelled at it (though this was not a reproach that greatly affected them). In certain forms of worship, cult-objects, such as the flowers, are said to have spiritual equivalences; all the objects of external array become symbols. In this way, any stretch of water can represent the Ganges for the real believer. The initiate offers the divinity the lotus of his heart as a seat, his thoughts as an oblation, the ambrosia that flows from the lotus of the skull as water to wash his feet; this ambrosia acts as ablution, the breath as incense, the inward flame as a lamp. This is a development of the Vedic *prāṇāgnihotra*, the *Agnihotra* transformed into a sacrifice to the breath, in which the fire was replaced by the officiant's mouth, and the ritual offerings by homage to the five aspects of the breath and their correlatives in the microcosm and in the macrocosm. Substitutions are practised everywhere; thus in the theory of expiation, expiatory practices appropriate to each individual sin are painstakingly established, and are then replaced by general expiations, often purely theoretical in character, which overthrow the whole system. The famous *vratas*, religious 'observances', often fantastic in form and setting, also contain substituted features that have a symbolical basis.

The serpent that lies coiled inside the body, the *kuṇḍalinī*, is another of these fantasies, a hallucination produced by mystical ecstasy. The *kuṇḍalinī* myth is an aid to meditation; it is a myth of intimate experience, representing an experiment carried out by the subject on himself.

Meditation can also be induced without external aid, by the exercises of *Yoga*; its final state is that inward concentration called *samādhi*, which would be translated inadequately by 'contemplation', and incorrectly by 'ecstasy'. It is an ancient technique based on controlled breathing and more or less acrobatic postures, adapted to the uses of mysticism. Both the *kuṇḍalinī* and the more advanced exercises of *Yoga* have a representational function: they unwittingly reproduce the orgasm that accompanies the *unio mystica*, and the material manifestation of which is that outpouring of *amṛta* or *soma*, described to us in poetical terms.

Many of the features we have discussed belong rather to Tantrism than to normal Hinduism. They may be already inherent in ancient forms of belief, but it is Tantric practice that systematizes them and brings out their full significance. If we are to attempt to define Tantrism, we must avoid facile judgments of the type that compares it to some creeping disease gradually invading not only Hinduism, but Buddhism as well. In the view of Avalon[1] and others, it represents the full flowering of the religious spirit of India.

Tantrism is based on a code of esoteric practices. In the extreme forms of it, at any rate, sexual representations, elsewhere stifled or confined to mythology, are much in evidence, as in the *pañcatattva*, which consists in approaching woman, newly dignified as *śakti*, by means of the five '*m*'s', *madya*, *māṃsa*, *matsya*, *mudrā*, *maithuna*. Such doctrines were no doubt of limited application, and their manifest dangers were guarded against by careful discrimination in the initiation of new adherents; the initiation process might be either slow, semi-slow, rapid, or instantaneous, the merits of instantaneous initiation being considered sufficient to bring the neophyte to the verge of Liberation.

In the broader sense of the term Tantrism may be defined as a technique designed to revitalize current practice and make it more expressive and more effective. By bringing divergent tendencies to a head and by introducing new trends of its own, the movement may be said to have infused new life into Hinduism and to have saved its practices from becoming stereotyped. It is probably responsible for the vigorous condition of many sects today, and to some extent for the very survival of Hinduism.

[1] Cf. Arthur Avalon, *Principles of Tantra* (London, 1914–16); *Shakti and Shâkta* (London and Madras, 2nd edition, 1920), etc.

Tantrism, like all India's religious manifestations, has its own philosophy, a combination of *Sāṃkhya* and *Vedānta*; its cosmogony is dominated by the concept of *śakti*, the divine energy proceeding from the supreme Śiva. From *śakti* proceeds *bindu*, the mystical drop which develops the component elements of the universe; the system is still an esoteric one, of the *Sāṃkhya* type. According to the *Gopālatāpanī Upaniṣad*, the universe proceeds from a *mantra*, the sun from one sound-unit, the moon from another. Coexistent with the tangible world is the world of sound, also sprung from the original *bindu*. There is a return to the old Vedic correlations, which are given dynamic form, and are conceived not as the products of reflection but of intimate experience. In Tantric mythology an important part is played by female divinities, chief among whom is the Goddess, appearing in many forms. The rôle of creator belongs to her, the universal Wife and Mother, or to the *śakti* that proceeds from her, in face of Śiva's immobility.

Tantrism proposes its own path of Liberation. There is an essential distinction between the 'path of the right' (or right-hand path) and the 'path of the left' (or left-hand path). The method of the path of the right is the usual one of *Yoga* and *bhakti*: Pott, who has recently made a study of Tantric *Yoga*, says: 'Here the union with the All-Highest is aspired to in an emotional-dynamic sense: in an individual effort to arrive at the elimination of the duality subject-object, this *Yoga* knows of a self-abnegation, a blissfulness in which the soul—passive itself—is lifted up by the divine grace, and in which form of *Yoga* there is the possibility of a union born and growing in a state of ecstasy.'[1] This is *Śrīvidyā*, or 'sacred knowledge'; it is also called *Layayoga*, the *Yoga* of absorption, an expression that refers to the rite or inward myth of the *kuṇḍalinī*, and the break-

[1] P. H. Pott, *Yoga en Yantra in hunne Beteekenis voor de Indische Archaeologie* (Leiden, 1946). Quoted from the *résumé* in English, p. 157.

ing through the six circles of the body, which is the characteristic feature of this doctrine. It is only the imagery that is Tantric; in other respects it is not so much Tantrism proper as Tantric *bhakti*; the essential element is the presence and co-operation of the divine.

The 'path of the left' is very different, for there man must rely on his own efforts. To become an *avadhūta*, a man who has 'shaken off' the passions, sense-impressions must be, not temporarily suspended, as in *Yoga*, but intensified, so that man may realize the emptiness of the pleasure they arouse. For the *Yoga* of asceticism is substituted a *Yoga* of indulgence, *Bhoga*. It is a complete reversal of the usual values: 'fair is foul, and foul is fair' might be its motto. 'A thorn can be plucked out with another thorn', as one of the Tantric texts says. In a sense it is an easy path, for, says the *Guhyasamāja*, 'perfection can be attained easily by satisfying all the desires'. But there are many dangers; man cannot follow this path without preparation, which is not made available to all. 'The enjoyment of wine, food and women is the salvation of him who has understanding.' *Ya evaṃ veda*: already in the *Brāhmaṇas* this was the password that gave access to all that religion had to offer. To quote Pott once more, 'when following the "left path" the *sādhaka* strives after the destruction of the individual ego by concentrating on destroying the elements out of which the ego has been built up'.[1] The main purpose is to disintegrate the personality, by a process of bringing compelling influence to bear on the subject and of impressively staged imitation, which is in fact magic. As in the macabre forms of popular *abhicāra*, the favourite setting is the place of cremation, the cemetery where the material body is destroyed; demoniac conceptions are brought into play. The term *samādhi* is interpreted as 'place of death' by the Vīraśaivas, who profess a similar Tantrism. The central

[1] Op. cit., p. 159.

figure of the cult is Bhairava, the terrible aspect of Śiva, with his assistants. Bhairava's seat is the eight-petalled lotus; each petal supports one of the eight aspects of the god, and is also connected with the human body and its characteristic features; this is the lotus of the heart, the *Hṛdayapuṇḍarīka*, that appears in Purāṇic literature. The supreme liturgy is the sexual act, varied by all kinds of practices which need not be described in detail.

Although these doctrines are esoteric, they are also democratic, for they do not recognize distinctions of caste or sect: they are a kind of freemasonry. Men are classified according to their degree of qualification, the stage they have reached, and the good opinion of their *guru*: the *guru* has an important part in all these mystery cults for which an exacting initiation is required. There are the *paśus* or 'beasts' who understand only the rites of the right-hand path, or who, if they are admitted to those 'of the left', only practise them in altered form. Then there are the 'heroes', who follow the path of the left, either secretly, or, if they have reached a very exalted stage, openly. Sometimes an even higher category is recognized, the 'divine'; they are those who have transcended ritual obligations and concern themselves only with the symbols. They are the equivalent of the 'liberated-in-life' of other doctrines.

We are not yet ready to seek for the origins of Tantrism. The germ of the movement has been sought, and consequently found, in the Veda, as is so often the case with Indian problems which really have no beginning. Tantric correlations are, in fact, clearly connected with the old equivalences of the Vedic world; its magical and cosmogonic background suggests that of the *Atharvaveda*, in which arbitrary linguistic signs and 'veiled language' already appear. But this only shows that Tantrism may have had a shadowy prehistory and that it may contain very ancient material. Its system is new, however, and we do not know what events led to its formulation, nor whether it is of purely Indian origin or made up from miscellaneous sources external to Hinduism. Even the genetical connection between Hindu Tantrism and Buddhist Tantrism, or *Vajrayāna*, is far from being established. We can only observe that it grew up, not within Hinduism as a whole, but in the sects, in Śaivite rather than in Vaiṣṇavite circles, and in Śākta sects even more than in Śaivite ones. The general fictional setting is Śaivite-Śākta; it takes the form of a dialogue between Śiva and Pārvatī, in which the Goddess alternately asks questions as a pupil, and answers as a teacher the questions put by the god. These two forms of exposition were called by the old terms *Nigama* and *Āgama*. The dialogue form was inspired by the *Purāṇas*, where it is constantly used; it is also found in the *Adhyātmarāmāyaṇa* and in Tulsīdās.

Nowhere in the world is there a system of speculative thought, or rather, a representation of mystical truth, that is more radical or more paradoxical in form than Tantrism. India has shown that, as M. Éliade says, 'man can transcend his mortal condition with equal success by the way of Asceticism, or by its polar opposite, the way of Eroticism. They both lead him to the same condition: freedom from contingency, the state of the liberated in life, the man-god.'[1]

[1] *Techniques du Yoga* (Paris, 1948), p. 213.

V

Hinduism : III

HINDUISM, which we have so far studied as a single entity, now appears as a mosaic of sects and independent groups that are sometimes in rivalry; not that the total number of Hindu believers has ever been represented by the total membership of the sects, for this is far from being the case. Though no statistics are available, even for the present day, we have grounds for supposing that the most active sects were themselves only isolated groups within the great body of believers. This great mass is called by a name that distinguishes them from the sectarians; they are Smārtas, people who follow the tradition of *Smṛti*, of the *Purāṇas*, in other words the Ancients; one might almost say the orthodox, if that did not imply that the rest were heterodox. The Smārtas, too, seem to have gradually taken over sectarian features: they adopted a special form of *pūjā*, for example.

Yet the sects are alive and pertinacious. They often give evidence of a real effort to contest the laxness of existing religion, and to revive its discipline; but occasionally their object is to make religion more human and accessible. Most of the great men of Hinduism have been founders of sects and reformers. But for the sects, Hinduism would have had no internal history; the subject will therefore delay us a little.

Sects arise more readily in religions which have no clearly defined dogma; for there is then no risk of heresy in a personal preference for one special book or one special form of worship, or in individual variations in points of detail. Sects are sometimes just as radical as movements that declare themselves as unequivocally outside Hinduism: the Vīraśaivas are in some respects less Hindu than the modern Jainas, for they have cast aside more elements of the common heritage. The Mānbhāvs of the Marathi country have retained practically nothing of Hinduism; they minimize the importance of all the gods except Kṛṣṇa and Dattātreya; they despise *śruti* and avoid the temples; and yet despite the fear or scorn they inspire, they do not feel themselves to be excluded from the community. The fact seems to be that since Buddhism, which has long since disappeared from India, and Jainism, which shows a tendency to return to the fold of Hinduism, there have been no heresies and no serious schism even, unless the rival trends of Teṅgalai and Vaḍagalai within the Śrīvaiṣṇavas can be counted as such. The old heresies of the time of the Buddha seem to have been reabsorbed into the general background. The 'reformed sects', to use Farquhar's phrase,[1] that is the Kabīrpanthīs, the Sikhs and a few others, are on the borderline of Hinduism, rather than outside it. It is notable that all these movements sprang from Vaiṣṇavism; Śaivism, although apparently more extremist, has always been on the whole more conservative of tradition. Kabīr rejects ritual and Brahmanical speculation, but retains certain basic beliefs, such as *karman* and *saṃsāra*; he teaches of *māyā*, reserves the name Rāma or Hari for the Supreme Being, recognizes the divinization of the *guru* and the efficacy of repeating the divine Name. The Sikhs, who took over some of the features of Kabīr's 'religion', consider themselves as a separate sect on political rather than religious grounds. Nevertheless, they have established a Bible of their own, the *Granth*, composed on

[1] J. N. Farquhar, *An Outline of the Religious Literature of India* (London, 1920), p. 330.

the model of the *Ṛgveda*; in inspiration it resembles the *Gītā*, and its general principles are *bhakti* and divine grace. Both Kabīr and the Sikhs are the spiritual descendants of Rāmānanda, an ascetic whose reforms seem to have been motivated as much by social as by religious considerations, for he made the vernacular the medium of preaching (as the Buddha had previously done), and received low castes and outcastes into his community, as well as women. It has been suggested also that there may be some connection between these movements and the Nāths, who practise a Śaivism based on *Yoga*, possibly the *Haṭhayoga*. Tradition has it that there was a personal contact between Gorakhnāth and Kabīr or Nānak.

How, then, can an Indian sect be defined? Some features, such as the wearing of certain emblems, are merely superficial. Adherence to a particular sacred book and to a particular divinity is more decisive. This does not mean that there is a sect attached to each member of the pantheon; the *Purāṇas* which express allegiance to Viṣṇu or Śiva are not for that reason the manifesto of any particular sect. In effect, the sects of India are divided into two groups, Vaiṣṇavite and Śaivite; the Śākta movements can be regarded as an independent development with a Śaivite background. We must also take into account the evidence that a community giving allegiance to the Sun-god, the Sauras or Saurapatas, existed in ancient times; the movement may well have been associated with the rise of a solar cult brought from Iran, or at any rate promoted by Iranian influence. There are also traces of a group paying devotion to Gaṇeśa, which is thought to have flourished between the sixth and eighth centuries; but this may have been an esoteric tendency superimposed on other beliefs.

Adherence to a particular sacred book does not necessarily imply innovation; it is more common to draw upon the past than to invent anew. But it often happens that the poems or sermons of the founder are regarded as a new Canon, as with the *Granth* of the Sikhs, which was venerated like an eleventh *guru*. The Caitanya devotees have an oral literature, attributed to their leader; the written works, the six *Saṃdarbhas*, are little more than a theological commentary. Some books are common to many sects, among them several *Upaniṣads*, the *Bhagavadgītā* and the *Bhāgavatapurāṇa*, which few Indians reject. The Śivanārāyaṇīs, a movement of the eighteenth century, assert that their scriptures are of great antiquity, and that they were incomprehensible until an inspired ascetic translated them. Every group makes similar efforts to prove that it is of ancient origin; this is a typically Indian tendency, shown in the efforts made by the composers of the Epic and all the great texts of antiquity to build up a conjectural structure, starting with a revealed Ur-text, existing from time immemorial, which was lost, recovered later, and summarized, this summary in its turn being lost and resummarized, and so on. In other texts, a mythical sage is claimed as author, so that a whole literature takes on an apocryphal aspect.

Each sect also adopts a philosophical standpoint of its own; that is to say, it takes up a position in relation to the classical *Vedānta* and *Sāṃkhya*; in addition, it has something to contribute to a theory of cosmology. It must be admitted that we know nothing of the speculative thought of certain groups; it is possible that those who developed none disappeared the more easily for that very reason. In this connection, it should be noted that the Śaṅkaran *Vedānta* is not connected with any sect and that none of them directly adopted it. It is true that the Smārtas pass for Śaṅkarans, but I think it more likely that this is because of the religious foundations attributed to Śaṅkara than because of his philosophical activities. Neither is the *Sāṃkhya* in its pure state the subject of sectarian speculation. No doubt these systems were too rigid and had too little hold over the masses. On the other hand, the theistic *Sāṃkhya* and the non-Śaṅkaran *Vedānta* provided the doctrinal basis of a series of religious movements, a fact which emphasizes the important part played by *bhakti* in the development of the sects. It was by means of *bhakti* that they were able to sway the tendencies of philosophical doctrine; there is no sect without some element of *bhakti*.

There is not necessarily any organized religious system within these groups. Hinduism has no sense of hierarchy; the monastic communities, the essence of Buddhism and Jainism, were not widely imitated in this respect. India early established the categories of mendicant monk, anchorite, and ascetic, and on this foundation built up the *āśramas*, in the old sense of the term, which designates the divisions of human existence. But it is not until the ninth century that the first traces of a Hindu order appear, allegedly founded by Śaṅkara, with its ten brotherhoods, its regional directors, and its supreme head who bears the reverential title of *jagadguru*. Later there is mention of monasteries founded by the Vīraśaivas, by several Vaiṣṇavite sects (notably by Rāmānuja at Śrīraṅgam and Melkote), and even by the Kabīrpanthīs. The inscriptions of the South give details of the practical organization of the *maṭhas* and sanctuaries from the thirteenth century onwards; under the Pāṇḍyas there are references to the Ekadaṇḍins, elsewhere to the Tridaṇḍins. But all this amounts to very little, and the history of Hindu monachism, if it can be said to have a history, has yet to be written.

Finally, a sect cannot be founded without personal initiative. Of course, there are movements that do not claim one man as their founder, and others, like the Pāśupatas and the Kāṇphaṭins, that trace their origin to legendary figures. But there must have been an historical basis on which the legendary element was superimposed; we must bear in mind the recognized Indian tendency to confuse the facts as time goes on. There are many similarities in the historical origins of the various sects, and the biographies of their holy men present many examples of reduplication. The correspondences between the Buddha and Mahāvīra have caused much surprise, but there are other similar cases. The usual pattern is as follows: at a certain point in his life a man cuts himself off from his normal surroundings, though nothing in his former ways or in his heredity predisposed him to this action; he receives illumination; he goes forth to preach a new doctrine, and introduces new practices; he meets with many difficulties and sometimes with persecution. He finally succeeds in forming a group of disciples, laymen as well as religious devotees, and he designates one of them to be his successor. This is not a universal legend, however, for there were no founders of cults in Greece.

The Master either commits his doctrine to writing himself, or his words are recorded by someone else. Caitanya and Rāmānanda, who left virtually no literary record, are isolated cases; and their disciples have largely made good the deficiency. Cakradhara, who gathered the Mānbhāvs together, is a semi-legendary founder; the son of a minister, he led the life of a libertine and died at twenty-five. Then, just as Śaṅkara entered into the body of King Amaru to learn the *ars amandi* (the only discipline of which he was ignorant), so the soul of Srī Gāṅgadeva passes into Cakradhara's body, and he returns to life; then, after a personal sorrow, the death of his wife, he becomes an ascetic, founds a community, and ends his days in the Himālayas. The lives of Lakulīśa and Gorakhnāth contain features that are even more fanciful. But the legends are usually built up round some definite locality, and have some factual basis that can be corroborated.

The founder and his successors may become the objects of a personal cult, which is sometimes carried to great lengths. This fact can be explained without reference to extra-Indian influences, for it has always been a feature of Tantrism. Perhaps the first historical evidence of it is the divinization of the Tamil 'saints' under the Cōḷas. The followers of Caitanya eventually exalted their master to such a degree that he almost eclipses Kṛṣṇa. In the case of the Vallabhācāryas, whose hereditary leader is a *guru* directly descended from the founder, worship of this type caused considerable scandal in the eighteenth century. The conception of *avatāras* facilitated the process of deification. For many Hindus nothing could be more dangerous than the abolition of images: they put the living *guru* in their place.

Sectarian teaching, by definition, aims at reform. On the one hand, a sect preaches the purification of religion, renunciation of images and of animal sacrifice; in this way it provides a check to the natural drift of religious practice. Some groups emphasize the need for asceticism, because their dominant element is composed of *saṃnyāsins*. On the other hand, a sect may aim at making a wider appeal to the masses, may protest against esotericism and caste distinctions, and demand that the texts shall be made more easily understandable and that preaching shall be in the vernacular; in the eleventh century, for example, the Liṅgāyats, before the time of Basava, composed sermons in Kanarese, the *vacanas*. It may be surmised that the sects played an important part in the spread of Indian dialects. But it may also happen, as in the case of the Mānbhāvs, that a sect favours a greater degree of esotericism, and adopts secret writings. Finally it must be noted that certain little-known movements came into being under stimulus from outside, though as yet we have little information on this subject; it is certain, however, that the Vaiṣṇavite

Sahajīyas of Bengal were influenced by Buddhism; the Bengali cult of Dharma was influenced by Buddhist Tantrism; and there is a current of crypto-Buddhism among the Śaivite or Śākta Nāths. It is more than probable, too, that there is an Islamic element in the Dharma cult and in the Bengali Bāuls (Bengal was certainly the region most exposed to outside influence), as well as in Kabīr and the Sants. But the basis of all these movements is indisputably Hindu.

The attitude of the sects to the caste-system must also be considered. There is no evidence of any serious revolt against the system as such; but there is insistence that all members have equal religious rights; otherwise no true community would be possible. The disintegration of caste-barriers is brought about indirectly, by the establishment of a new scale of values. Caitanya, who is supposed to have preached universal brotherhood, displays a guarded attitude to caste; the initiation of a man belonging to one of the three highest classes is not undertaken by a *śūdra* master. Certain groups draw their membership from one professional class; the Rāidāsīs, for example, are tanners, and the Sadhanpanthīs are butchers. The tanner caste of Cāmars tended to form a sect on their own. It is said that there is no intermarriage between the two Śrīvaiṣṇava schools, the Teṅgalai of the south and the Vaḍagalai of the north, although it is only a theological dispute that separates them. The Vīraśaivas have a body of hereditary priests, the *jaṅgamas* or '*liṅgas* in motion': and hereditary privilege leads eventually to the caste-system.

We are also faced with the problem of deciding when the sects arose. It would be tempting to suppose that the *Upaniṣads* were the products of schools that were in the process of developing into sects: it was the speculations of these groups of adherents to a particular form of ritual that came to be known as the Vedic *śākhās*. But this theory, though not improbable in itself, would be somewhat arbitrary. On the other hand, the only example of a school developing into a sect is provided by one of these *śākhās*, that of the Vaikhānasas of the *Yajurveda*; but it would be possible to see this as a case of the reverse procedure of a community of ascetics styling themselves a *śākhā*; however this may be, the Vaiṣṇavite *Saṃhitā* of the Vaikhānasas is a direct continuation of the *Kalpasūtra* of the same name. But let us consider the subject in more general terms: we know that there were devotees of Viṣṇu and Śiva at a fairly early date; inscriptions attest dynastic nomenclatures that are sometimes Vaiṣṇavite and sometimes Śaivite in style. This does not necessarily imply the existence of clearly defined groups. It is true that in the Epics and later works specific names are found, such as the Pāśupatas, and the Bhāgavatas referred to in the second century B.C. by Heliodorus, who was the ambassador of the Greek King Antalikhita (Antialkidas), to the ruler of Besnagar, Bhāgabhadra of the Śuṅga dynasty. But we cannot be certain that the references are to sects; the texts are not explicit on the point. Rāmaism emerges as an independent movement only at a late period, but the cult of Rāma is an ancient one; there are surely grounds for the supposition that Rāmaist groups existed in ancient times. Similarly, the Śākta cult must also be ancient, although the Śākta sects are of comparatively recent formation. But nothing is really known of the history of the sects before the end of the tenth century, or in the South perhaps a little earlier; the history of Śaivism can be traced back slightly further. The essential doctrines are well established at this period, and the sects have reached the stage of revivifying speculations that have become outworn.

It is clear that Śaivism is related on the one hand to *Nyāya-Vaiśeṣika*, and on the other hand to *Yoga*. Śiva is the central figure in the mythological background of the

Yoga mystery and a Śaivite atmosphere was favourable to its development; it is only at a late period that there is any Śaivite adherence to the *Vedānta*, and then it was confined to Śrīkaṇṭha's movement. Śaivism attaches great importance to the practices, especially to asceticism (the majority of ascetics are Śaivites), but it values *bhakti* less highly; it leans towards esotericism. It is interesting to note that it was Śaivism that gained the firmest foothold in Eastern Asia, and produced a vast body of speculative literature principally in Old Javanese; according to Zieseniss,[1] this literature represents a stage earlier than that of the *Śaivasiddhānta* of Southern India. It was Śaivism that profited most by the expulsion of Buddhism and the decline of the Jainas. The Vaiṣṇavite movements do not definitely take the lead until the eleventh century, when *bhakti* comes into prominence, and under the personal impetus of Rāmānuja, which seems to have been a decisive factor. At this period, too, Vaiṣṇavism predominates in Cambodia and in other parts of South-East Asia; there is a remarkable degree of coincidence between the ebb and flow of these movements on the Indian mainland and in the countries to which Hinduism has spread. At the present time, Vaiṣṇavism is generally predominant, except in Bengal where the Śāktas have retained their hold. Ritual is less in evidence in Vaiṣṇavism than in Śaivism (though it is not altogether lacking, as has been supposed); and Vaiṣṇavism is in general milder and purer in form; there is no trace of the crude and semi-barbaric features of the Śiva cult. The extreme aspects of Tantrism are less apparent in it, and its contribution to literature is greater; nearly all the great religious works are Vaiṣṇavite, and there is on the whole a close correspondence between doctrine and cult.

[1] Studien zur Geschichte des Śivaismus: die Śivaitischen Systeme in der altjavanischen Literatur', *I. Bijdr. Taal-, Land-, Volkenk. Ned-Ind.*, 98 (1939), p. 74.

The existence of these sects side by side has, of course, given rise to controversy and to a kind of endemic rivalry; and all the sects present a common front against Śaṅkara. But there have been few violent clashes, and little or no persecution; if the Mānbhāvs and the Vīraśaivas found themselves in trouble, it was because of the intractability of their behaviour in society rather than because of their beliefs. Tolerance prevails; or perhaps it should be called indifference. Caitanya was an adept of *bhakti*, and an *advaitin* at the same time, like Śrīdhara; Śaṅkara himself was a devotee of Śiva; Appayadīkṣita, a Smārta who was converted to Śāktism, composed commentaries on both Śaivite and Vaiṣṇavite works. The administration of the temples may have given rise to local clashes, but these were not directly connected with sectarian adherence; the inscriptions of the Pāṇḍyas mention quarrels of precedence and so on in the thirteenth century.

I shall now attempt a brief historical survey of Hinduism, along the lines I have indicated.

As we have seen, there are grounds for supposing that some form of Hinduism existed at the Vedic period, and probably even earlier. This is the prehistory of Hinduism; its history begins with the emergence of the great texts of Hindu *dharma*, and the first appearance of the Epic and of *Smṛti*. At this point Hindu belief achieves a status of its own; there is an effort to define its position in relation to Vedic practice, just as there was a definition of the status of the Pāṇinean *bhāṣā* in relation to the *chandas*. The same period saw the origins of Buddhism and Jainism; a survey of the allusions to Hinduism in the heretical Canons would be of great interest. The Buddha attacks caste prejudices and the proud attitude of the Brahmans, but he scarcely touches on the fundamentals of belief; in the *Tevijja-Sutta* he asks how the god Brahman whom no one has ever seen can be an object of worship; but the cult of Brahman was one of those practically unknown to Hinduism. There is virtually no general attack on Hindu practices, except on bloody sacrifices, which are condemned in the name of *ahiṃsā*. The Jaina Canon refers to a large body of ascetics; the Pāli Canon alludes to intensive speculative activity, and disputes between sophists, agnostics and determinists; it implies a background not unlike that of the oldest *Upaniṣads*. But the evidence is not sufficient to give us any clear idea of the state of contemporary Hinduism; we are led to the conclusion that it was in large measure tacitly accepted. The Jaina critique was perhaps more emphatic, and certainly continued longer; we find examples of it in Siddharṣi, in Devasena, and as late as the tenth century in Somadeva, who criticizes the sects and schools. But these attacks had become in some measure a literary convention.

After the decline of Vedism, the official religion was at first Buddhism, under the Mauryas. Nothing is known of the Hinduism of this period; it is only when an ancient Indian religion is adopted as the State religion that we have any real knowledge of it, for from then on there is evidence of it in public ceremonial, in inscriptions and on coins, in monuments, and in court poetry and panegyrics. It is said that a reaction took place under the Śuṅgas, and again a little later under the Āndhras, because certain of these kings restored the Vedic sacrifices. But this is a very slight piece of evidence. My view is that the people of India as a whole must always have been Hindu; they did not have to be won back from Buddhism, which, in spite of royal patronage, was from the start more or less confined to monasteries and schools. It is true that royal protection was accorded to Buddhism at several subsequent periods, under the Indo-Greeks at the time of Menander, and under the Kuṣāṇas, or at any rate under Kaniṣka in the first or second century A.D.; in other words, under foreign rulers. It is a pity that the Hindu dynasties of the pre-

Gupta period did not pay such explicit testimony to their faith. We have only the barest indications to guide us: the inscription of Ghusuṇḍi, dating from about 150 B.C., mentions the construction of a building to the glory of Saṃkarṣaṇa and Vāsudeva; there are the Śaivite coins of Gondophares a century and a half later; soon after this, the title of *maheśvara* is assumed by Kadphises and there is a Śaivite coinage under Vāsudeva. But we cannot gather a great deal from this, even when taken in conjunction with the inscription of Heliodorus already cited, and the general observations of Megasthenes on Indian beliefs of the fourth century B.C. There are no grounds for assuming, as some writers do, that Bhāgavatism flourished in Northern India between the fourth and second centuries B.C., and was then superseded by Śaivism under members of the Kuṣāṇa dynasty. We have slightly fuller inscriptional evidence of the spread of Kṛṣṇaism in Central India from the first or perhaps the second century B.C.

With the Gupta dynasty, in the early fourth century, the position changes. This great indigenous dynasty was the first to support the whole body of Indian orthodoxy; the first Guptas called themselves *paramabhāgavatas*; they were the patrons of the Brahmans and of Hindu communities; mentions of schools and sects begin to be found. Moreover, we know that under the Guptas Sanskrit, which had probably been for some time the language of administration, came to maturity as a literary medium. This may have helped to strengthen the Hindu faith, together with the rise of an architectural style of non-Buddhist inspiration at the same period. But all the same we must beware of talking of this as a Hindu renaissance, in the manner of scholars in the past. No renaissance of Hinduism was possible because it never died out, or even diminished in strength; the fact is simply that at this period conditions were so favourable to it that the traces it left behind are unusually conspicuous. The development of Tantrism and the Śākta doctrines may be tentatively ascribed to the end of the Gupta period. The testimony of Fa-Hien and others seems to indicate that the attitude to Buddhism was friendly; this attitude is epitomized in the eclecticism of Harṣa in the first half of the seventh century. Nevertheless, the decline of Buddhism, as attested, for example, by Hiuen-Tsang, must have involved some violent feelings: the official urbanity of the great monarchies was one thing; the uncompromising attitude of the sects and local groups quite another. But whatever the circumstances of the change were, from this time onwards most of the dynasties are Hindu; Vaiṣṇavism predominates under the ancient Cālukyas; then, from the seventh century onwards, Śaivism takes the lead, even under foreign rulers like the Hephtalites; their adherence to Śiva has been explained by M. Ghirshman as the result of a secondary identification of Śiva with Mithra.[1]

The period from 700 to 1200, which Vincent Smith terms the Rājput period,[2] also saw the Moslem conquest. In the field of speculation, it is the time of the great commentators, chief among them Kumārila and Śaṅkara. To them is due the final defeat of Buddhism, in a campaign inaugurated in the South by the zeal of the Tamil 'saints', the Vaiṣṇavite Āḷvārs and the Śaivite Nāyanārs. At this period Dravidian religion begins to assume characteristic form: the conception of 'saints' is developed; a certain religious syncretism appears; and perhaps now also the first sects emerge in the form of independent, clearly-defined communities. In the South, too, the first religious persecutions took place from the seventh century onwards, that of the Vīraśaivas in the Telugu country and of the Śrīvaiṣṇavas

[1] R. Ghirshman, *Les Chionites-Hephtalites* (Cairo, 1948), p. 57.

[2] Cf. *The Early History of India*, etc. (Oxford, 1904); *The Oxford History of India* (Oxford, 1919).

in the Tamil country. This outbreak of fanaticism is directed not only against the Buddhist and Jaina heresies but on occasion against fellow Hindus: the Cōḷas, who were Śaivites, persecuted Rāmānuja, who had to take refuge in flight. There are isolated cases where a man like Vemana constitutes himself the violent opponent of ritual and of the external show of the cult; Śaivism at this time produced the influential doctrines of *Siddhānta* in Southern India, and *Trika* in Kashmir, though it is impossible to say whether these systems were associated with active groups. Śaivism is also manifested in crude forms, such as the Kāpālikas, Kālāmukhas, and so on, and the Vīraśaivas and Liṅgāyats round about the twelfth century; Śaivism predominates in the Deccan: the Jaina Somadeva, in the tenth century, knows nothing of the Vaiṣṇavite sects. Towards the twelfth century *bhakti* is developed under the influence of Rāmānuja, and in a more popular, or at any rate a more picturesque form in the *Bhāgavatapurāṇa*, the date of which is uncertain. The great Vedic sacrifices were rarely performed, as Al-Bīrūnī attests, but the authority of the Veda was constantly reaffirmed, by Kumārila and the composers of the *Nyāya-Vaiśeṣika* on the speculative level, and on the practical level by the Smārtas, though there is no agreement as to when and where the latter came to the fore. Religious activity was centred round the great shrines, at any rate in the South, and, as has already been pointed out, the ninth century saw the establishment of the first monasteries, which were to find the Śaivite regions of the South particularly favourable to their development.

The following period may be said to continue until the end of the eighteenth century without spectacular change; during this time religious commentaries followed close upon one another in all branches of knowledge. The Śaṅkaran *Vedānta* in particular makes enormous strides, and moves by imperceptible stages towards a doctrine of theism; other forms of the *Vedānta*, said to be Vaiṣṇavite, emerge under Madhva, Nimbārka, and Vallabha, among others. The development of Tantrism continues, especially in Bengal where it tends to merge with the Śākta cult, which was firmly established there from at least the fourteenth century onwards. *Bhakti* is most commonly associated with Vaiṣṇavism (Kṛṣṇaism), as it was from the beginning, but from the fifteenth century at least it is also associated with Rāmaism; wave after wave of masters and poets contribute to its growth. The sects reached the zenith of their development between the thirteenth and mid-sixteenth centuries; after this period devotional *smārta* becomes dominant or regains its power in many regions. From the fifteenth century onwards, an important feature is the syncretism of Kabīr, and the rise of the 'reformed sects', such as the Sikhs, which seems to have been due to his influence. Religious literatures are developed, the Marathi from the end of the thirteenth century, the Bengali from the fourteenth century, and the Hindi from the fifteenth century; the Dravidian literatures, the Tamil hymns and panegyrics at least, go back much further. On the question of Islamic influence, we have already mentioned the existence of mixed sects and of sects arising from Sūfī impulsion, but these have only a very limited following; reference has also been made to the Islamic persecutions, which resulted on the one hand in the defection of a considerable number of Hindu adherents (especially those who did not belong to active sects) from their ancestral faith, and on the other hand in a strengthening of Hindu solidarity and in a more rigorous enforcement of religious practices and precepts. There were two main periods of persecution, under Fīrūz in the fourteenth century and under Sikander II and the Lodis in the fifteenth; the reign of Akbar in the sixteenth century was marked by a period of tolerance, but under Aurangzeb in the seventeenth century the attack was renewed; it led to a peasant revolt, and the rise and subsequent destruction of a semi-military sect, the Satnāmīs; Aurangzeb forbade the tonsure, closed down the *ghaṭs* and destroyed the shrines of Mathurā. The figures of Sūrdās and Tulsīdās in the sixteenth and seventeenth centuries epitomize the yearning for a consolidation of the living forces of Hinduism in Northern India to meet the threat of Moslem oppression.

The period from the eighteenth century onwards is often characterized as one of decline, because of the falling off of inspiration both in literature and doctrine, and the decadence of the Sanskrit substructure and of traditional learning. Of course, this decline, if such it was, barely touched the Hinduism of the people; it did not preclude local revivals such as the Śāktist revival in Bengal, and the upsurge of religious patriotism in the Marathi country. But at this time it seemed likely that the influence of Western civilization and the increased activity of Christian missions, especially in the South, would eventually alter the face of Indian religion.

But in the nineteenth century an important change took place. The awakening of nationalistic feeling gave rise to, or at any rate encouraged certain movements that favoured a return to tradition and were in reaction against the liberal ideas brought in from the West. Another factor of still greater importance was the succession of men of strong personality who came to the fore in various parts of India and gradually attracted the attention of cultured circles in all countries to what came to be known as the 'spirituality' of India. In fact, the West, on discovering these men and their achievements, endowed Indian spirituality with an importance that was disproportionate, not to its intrinsic value in the history of ideas, but to the extent of its influence in India and the numbers it affected.

The earliest of these men was a Bengali Brahman, Rām

Mohun Roy; he set himself the task of making his co-religionists give up crude practices such as idolatry and *satī*. Many previous teachers had made similar attempts, but his plan of campaign was different: he sent out a stream of skilful propaganda, tracts, newspaper articles and reviews, for he had a great talent for public relations. He deliberately adopted the Western scale of values, and cited Christian theology to prove the necessity of monotheism, which he declared to have existed also in ancient India. The group that he founded, the *Brāhmasamāj*, was a partly social and partly religious organization; in some respects it was not unlike the clubs of Western society. Rām Mohun emphasizes the necessity of far-reaching social reform; he seems to bring religion down to earth, as do also his successors and imitators: Keshab Chunder Sen, who, however, is too insistent in his desire to bring Hinduism closer to Christianity; Debendranāth Tagore, who, by contrast, intensified the traditionalist tendencies within Brāhmoism, as it came to be called; finally Mahādev Govind Rānaḍe, who emphasized social problems. The succession of movements for religious reform, which has continued right up to the present day, may be said to derive from Rām Mohun Roy. Gāndhi and Tagore are agreed on the necessity for bringing religion down to earth, however much they may differ on other points; and the 'Rāmakṛṣṇa Mission', which we in Europe and America know chiefly in its aspect as an organization for neo-Vedāntin propaganda, is in India itself principally concerned with educational and philanthropic work.

In the field of speculation, the writings and teaching of Rādhākṛṣṇan and Aurobindo Ghose may be considered as attempts to modernize Hinduism and to utilize its living power by adapting it to the needs of minds accustomed to Western theology and philosophy. Rādhākṛṣṇan eradicates from Indian forms all features that are peculiar to them, and builds them up into a symbolism that can be adapted to any form of religion. Aurobindo preaches a new syncretism based on a reinterpretation of the religious manifestations of India, from the Veda to Tantrism; the key to the future progress of humanity, he says, lies in India's past. In pursuance of this theory, he propounds a new interpretation of the great Sanskrit texts of antiquity, and at the same time develops new methods of *Yoga* in conformity with modern trends, in his *āśrama* at Pondicherry. Before him, Vivekānanda at the end of the last century had already attempted a re-interpretation of the *Vedānta*; using public oratory as his medium, he inculcated the theme of the unity of all religions, and spoke on this subject in person at the Congress of Religions in Chicago.

The example of Rāmakṛṣṇa may perhaps seem more striking to Europeans; he was a professed ascetic, with exceptional powers of mysticism; he was not a highly educated man, but he was firmly resolved to prove by personal experience that it was possible to attain mystical power through the medium of any form of the divine; and thus he prepared the way for a universal form of mysticism.

Some of these movements have been carried to extreme lengths. Keshab Chunder Sen, as we have seen, tried to christianize his sect; mention must also be made of Bāl Gaṅgadhār Tilak, the Marathi politician and philologist, whom his admirers call the father of Indian nationalism (he has also been called the father of Indian unrest); his passionate devotion to Hindu traditions led him to indulge in some of the most fantastic speculations that have ever appeared on the origins of Vedic civilization. There was also Dayānanda Sarasvatī, a Gujarāti ascetic, who founded the Āryasamāj: he was in favour of returning to an unqualified adherence to the Veda, and claimed that explicit principles of pure monotheism and of social and moral reform could be found in the hymns. As well as his work of religious reform and his eminent achievements as an exegete, he was active in urging that Hinduism must establish within itself a Church militant that should work unceasingly for political and social reform.

Rabīndranāth Tagore is probably the man whose work is best known in the West, and whose reputation seems most likely to last there. He too was a profoundly religious man, but he was without fanaticism; his humanistic culture made his religion enlightened and gentle. The synthesis he advocates, though today it is temporarily neglected, is still the one most likely to succeed, for it does not exact adherence prior to personal conviction. In Tagore's nature humaneness and poetic feeling are harmoniously united: in him the poet is at one with the religious thinker, the educationalist and the politician. Although he is a representative figure of the new India, he also exemplifies tendencies common to the most enlightened members of all communities. It is through him that great poets throughout the world are conscious of an intimate affinity with India.

I have neither the knowledge nor the inclination to prophesy what the future of Hinduism will be. Unless there is a radical social upheaval (which is within the bounds of possibility), it seems unlikely that the Hinduism of the people will greatly change; we have seen it to be inherent in India's evolution and in all the principles that have grown up around religion from time immemorial to form an indissoluble unity. People all too easily accuse religion of having contributed to economic and social depression. In many minds religion is automatically associated with privilege of class and caste, a fact that also tends to prejudice the survival of Sanskrit culture. If Hinduism can avoid this aspersion, it may be able to gain new vitality by enlisting the more enlightened classes in its service; for this it will need the leadership of a few men of strong personality to organize a movement of supporters and sympathizers. This will be an opportunity to see whether the machinery of a sectarian organization, which was so frequently and easily called into service in ancient India, is still capable of effective action, whether it is sufficiently flexible to avoid heightening the 'communalistic' tendencies which many Indians deplore.

Some people think that Hinduism should cease to be ethnical in character (assuming that it ever has been so), and become once more a missionary religion. There are already several organizations for spreading a knowledge of Hinduism in the West, but very often their propaganda does not reach the right circles. When Hinduism is 'exported', it tends to be regarded as a kind of theosophy —after all, the basic doctrinal principles of theosophy are rooted in Hinduism—or as a brand of Christian Science, tinged with pseudo-Vedāntism. It can only become a force for good in the world when it emerges in India itself as a purified form of religion, free from primitivism and the cult of images. Extreme practices, such as *Haṭhayoga* and Tantrism 'of the left', which often make such a deep impression on Europeans, never constitute the main strength of a religion; they are special features that should not be imitated outside the land of their origin.

As many Indians admit, Hinduism is greatly in need of a priesthood. The fact that there are no seminaries and, with a few exceptions, no monastic orders, has often been deplored. Indians observe, not without envy, that in Britain, for instance, many able men become ministers of religion on leaving the University, whereas in India there are no official religious leaders, but only solitary devotees working out their own salvation and preoccupied with an inward mystic revelation which they cannot communicate to others. If one wishes to get in touch with someone who officially represents Hinduism, it is very difficult to know whom to approach. The need for a Church is perhaps felt more acutely today than it has been in the past.

The troubles of the present age, which are rightly or wrongly attributed to Western materialism, have helped to increase the prestige of Hinduism. Some people see it as the authentic survival of a tradition, or rather, of the one Tradition, and make it the basis of their *philosophia perennis*. Others try to incorporate it in a universal religious syncretism. Whether these attempts will succeed must be left for the future to decide. The fact remains that Hinduism provides an incomparable field of study for the historian of religion: its aberrations are many, but there is in it a great stream of mystical power; it manifests all the conceptions of religion, and its speculation is continually revealing them in a new light. It combines powers of constant renewal with a firm conservancy of fundamental tradition. In *bhakti*, and still more in *Yoga*, it has perfected unrivalled techniques of mystical initiation, that contrast strongly with the frequently haphazard methods of spiritual training in the West. Above all, in the interpenetration of religion and *dharma* in general and the reciprocal stimulus of abstract thought and religious experiment, there is an underlying principle that, given favourable conditions, may well lead to a new integration of the human personality.

VI

Jainism

JAINISM has by no means aroused as much interest as Buddhism and Hinduism. It is practically unknown to the general public, despite the scholarly works that have been devoted to it, notably in Germany, but also in Great Britain and Italy. But if in the West there is little research at present being carried out in this field, in India, by contrast, where Buddhistic studies have never been very popular, the study of Jainism, especially of the post-Canonic period, has been widely pursued. Numerous societies have been formed to further Jainist studies, and collected editions of the texts have been issued by various bodies.

It must be admitted that Jainism does not at first sight seem to present the same general interest as Buddhism; the personality of its Founder is not so compelling; the texts are difficult, puzzling, and, frankly, tedious, as far as the non-specialist can judge them from translations, which are comparatively few in number. It is a religion of austere aspect, that might be described as Buddhism's darker reflection.

It was, in fact, its resemblance to Buddhism that most interested those who first investigated it. Several of these scholars held the theory that the Jainas were a sect that had separated from the early Buddhists. Others, basing their opinion on the fact that the Jainas could claim a slight chronological priority and that they even had some form of prehistory, considered Buddhism as an offshoot of Jainism.

Both of these movements are reformations directed

against Brahmanism, especially against the ritualistic aspect of it which predominated at the period, i.e. the sixth and fifth centuries B.C., when Vedism was on the wane. Their attack is, however, confined to the religious aspects of *dharma*, the Hindu Law; they accept the social order, or, at any rate, do not openly revolt against it. Both draw largely on the Hindu substratum for their teaching and the general framework of their systems.

One of the most important divergences between the two movements concerns the Master who originated the doctrine constituting the Jaina Canon, a doctrine that was at first oral in form, and was later written down. He is called the Great Hero or Mahāvīra, or sometimes the Victorious One or Jina (a name that is also occasionally bestowed on the Buddha), and he is described as the last of a sequence of prophets or patriarchs, stretching back to the remote past. Of course, ancient Buddhism also recognized earlier Buddhas, the obscure precursors of Śākyamuni, and the conception is more clearly formulated in the *Great Vehicle* with its doctrine of innumerable past and future Buddhas. But no definite dates are assigned to them, and there is no attempt at building up their life-histories.

In the Jaina system, then, we find the Tīrthaṃkaras, or 'forders' (a metaphor analogous to that of the Latin *pontifex*: the Romans use the image of a bridge, the Indians that of a ford). They are a coherent group of twenty-four men, who have attained Omniscience, and devote themselves to guiding humanity towards the true path. It should be noted that Buddhism also recognizes a group of twenty-five Buddhas, which could be taken as implying that Śākyamuni was the culmination of the sequence of twenty-four forerunners described in Jaina tradition.

The conception of the Tīrthaṃkaras is an ancient one; the iconography of Mathurā attests that it was current in the first century A.D. Of course, these legendary lives conform to a set pattern. The general outline is in accordance with a tradition that is automatically followed in descriptions of founders of sects in India: princely birth, sudden renunciation of the world as the result of 'illumination', and the founding of a community or body of disciples, one of whom becomes the successor. Of the symbolic details, some are identical with Buddhist forms (e.g. the tree sacred to each of the patriarchs), and some with Hindu forms, such as the associated animal, which is comparable with the 'mounts' of the Hindu divinities. The latter feature is post-Canonic, and so also is the conception of auxiliary divinities, frequently referred to in Buddhistic tradition, the Yakṣas and Yakṣiṇīs, who act as intercessors. An element of fantasy, fully consonant with the Jaina passion for numbers, appears in the matter of the great ages to which the Tīrthaṃkaras live: each one has a slightly shorter life than his predecessor. This feature was suggested by the Hindu *avatāras*. The Cakravartins or Universal Rulers, who are twelve in number, each one allegedly contemporary with two Tīrthaṃkaras (and who are also found in Buddhism with different associations), must surely have some connection with the Manus of Brahmanical theory, who are fourteen in number. Finally, the lives of the Tīrthaṃkaras are but elaborated versions of the life of Mahāvīra, the last of the sequence: not only is the general pattern the same, but even the details concerning the birth are identical, such as the fourteen dreams that come to the mother of each Tīrthaṃkara at the beginning of her pregnancy.

A slight variation in tone is perceptible, however, when we come to the twenty-second in the series, Nemi. Not that we approach historical fact (things do not progress as quickly as that in India); but his legend is more circumstantial than those of his predecessors; as in the case of the Buddha, there is a description of previous births. Even more remarkable is the traditional contemporaneousness of Nemi and the divine hero Kṛṣṇa. It has been pointed out that of the sixty-three 'great men' of Jaina prehistory, no less than twenty-seven had associations with Kṛṣṇa; Kṛṣṇaism seems to have left its mark on Jaina legend, a Kṛṣṇaism which we must assume (as we are frequently led to assume in the case of other Indian manifestations) to be an earlier form than that described in the Brahmanical texts. It has been suggested, somewhat daringly, that the legend of the Buddha is a reflection of that of Kṛṣṇa; if the theory of a Kṛṣṇaite association is to be retained, I should be more inclined to transfer it to the field of Jainism.

With the twenty-third Tīrthaṃkara, Pārśva, we are getting near to the historical period, if any meaning can be attached to the expression when dealing with this subject. It is a significant fact that the figures quoted in connection with him have been reduced to almost normal proportions. We are told that Pārśva died 250 years before Mahāvīra, for it is suspected that he founded a doctrine from which his successor drew his inspiration and which he 'reformed'. Mahāvīra's own parents are said to have been lay followers of Pārśva. It must be admitted that a multitude of fanciful suppositions have grown up around Pārśva. But all the same most scholars recognize him as the real founder. Mahāvīra was a great preacher who drew the crowds, but his contribution to doctrine seems to have been small. We are the more readily disposed to give credence to this theory because we are dealing with Indian material, and in India originality is far less highly valued than fidelity to tradition; but none the less it is possible that future research will show Pārśva's rôle to have been less significant. However this may be, Mahāvīra seems to have developed the ethical aspect of Jainism by introducing a fifth axiom which brought about a modification in the import of the fourth. He is said to have instituted the practice of confession.

Finally, it was he who required his monks to dispense with clothing, setting the example himself, whereas Pārśva's monks were clothed. The point may seem unimportant, but external details of this sort have always greatly exercised Indian sects; the problem of nakedness has in fact persisted in Jainism, and, as we shall see, has been the cause of a great schism that continues to the present day.

We now come to Mahāvīra, who is still called Vardhamāna, 'the growing one', an epithet of Vedic origin. Like Kṛṣṇa, he has a twofold birth, one in a Brahman family in Bihar—Bihar is the classic homeland of religious movements in ancient India—the other in a noble family, that of a clan chief in Magadha. In this way the sympathies of the two highest social classes are enlisted, albeit at the expense of physiological *vraisemblance*. Pelliot thought that there were too many kings' sons involved in these doctrines of renunciation.[1] True, but after all who, according to the Indian way of thinking, should renounce the world, if not those who have tasted all it has to offer?

The first coincidence emerges from a comparison of Jaina and Buddhist sources: the brother of the princess of Magadha, who was the mother of Mahāvīra, has a son-in-law, Seṇiya, who is none other than the Bimbisāra of Buddhist tradition, the father of Ajātaśatru, whom the Jainas call Kūṇiya.

Taken as a whole, Mahāvīra's life closely resembles the Buddha's. The general postulates, the pious aims of their biographers, the times and places are the same. Miraculous elements are not wanting, and are especially in evidence in accounts of the Master's birth; but even in recently compiled sources there is nothing comparable to the prodigality of Buddhism. The *Lalitavistara*, a poetical amplification of the theme of the Buddha's diversions, has no Jaina

[1] Cf. his preface to the French translation of H. v. Glasenapp's *Brahma und Buddha* (Berlin, 1926; French version, 1937).

counterpart. The typical ancient biography, the *Life of the Jina* by Bhadrabāhu, would find its closest parallel in Aśvaghoṣa's *Life of the Buddha.* The predestined child is brought up in princely splendour; he marries a girl of noble birth, a marriage not recognized by the more puritan of the two later branches of Jainism. By her he has a daughter who later marries. He leaves his family when his parents die (here there is a contrast with the Buddha); he enters upon a life of meditation and spends two years seeking the path; then he becomes a naked ascetic, vowed to the wandering life which he leads for twelve years. The element of asceticism is much more strongly stressed than in the case of the Buddha, who gave up the wandering life after six years.

In the thirteenth year he attains Omniscience; the revelation comes to him at the foot of a *śāla* tree, which is commemorated in the texts as a sacred tree (*caitya*). From that time onwards, the Master preaches the Law, tirelessly travelling round the Magadha-Aṅga-Videha region, training disciples, but also facing many demonstrations of hostility. He dies at the age of seventy-two, in the reign of Ajātaśatru, in a place called Pāvā, that the Jainas are probably wrong in supposing to be different from the Pāvā through which the Buddha was to pass soon afterwards in the course of his last journey.

The correspondences between Mahāvīra's life and that of the Buddha must spring from a common, pre-existing legendary source. Some of the common elements might just possibly have been derived from a third sect, that of the Ājīvikas, which seems to have exerted a noticeable influence on the other two. The leader of this sect, Gośāla Maṅkhaliputra, is said to have been a disciple of Mahāvīra for six years, after which he left him, attained the state of Jina and died sixteen years before Mahāvīra. He enjoined the practice of severe asceticism, especially in the matter of food, and developed the theory of *karman* (which he may have originated); this theory he carried to almost impossible lengths, denying free will and man's responsibility.

Western scholars date Mahāvīra's death in 467 or 477 B.C.; tradition puts it in 527. In any case it is after the Buddha's death, whether one accepts the date traditional in the South, 543, or the amended date, 483. In spite of this, a Pāli text states that the Jina died first; it probably suited the writer's purpose that the Buddha should survive longer.

Buddhist sources are scarcely more informative about the Jainas than Jainist sources are about Buddhism. They do mention the community of the Nirgranthas, 'those who have cast off their bonds', and their leader, whose name in Pāli is Nātaputta, and who has been plausibly identified with Mahāvīra. But they say virtually nothing about doctrine. It is difficult to realize how completely contemporary movements in India could be unaware of each other.

In spite of the difficulties and contradictions in the texts we are perhaps better informed about the early days of the Jaina community than about those of the Buddhist Church. We know that there were nine groups among the first disciples, with eleven group-leaders or heads; we know the names of those who recorded or transmitted the Master's words, the Theras or Ancients. The Jainas were acutely aware of the progressive attenuation of this knowledge; only the first two disciples are *kevalins*, full possessors of knowledge; and the history of Jainism has been characterized by the effort to retrace the path and rediscover the original sources of knowledge.

The most remarkable of these ancient religious leaders is Bhadrabāhu, the sixth Thera. He is the second most important figure in Jainism. He was contemporary with the first Maurya, and lived, therefore, in the fourth century B.C.; it fell to him to take the initiative in the famous migration to the South which was a flight from imminent famine. The story may have been invented subsequently to explain the Jaina colony in Mysore, and to give the support of orthodoxy to the doctrinal developments brought about by the exodus. At all events, it is suspicious that two versions of the story are found; according to the second version, the event took place under the principate of Sthūlabhadra, a disciple of Bhadrabāhu.

It is recounted that when these emigrants, or some of them at least, returned to the North, they found that there had been a relaxation of religious observances. In India, the people of the South have always been rather strict in such matters. In this way there arose a state of affairs conducive to schism, which, however, did not occur until much later, in 79 B.C. This seems to be the last of the seven heresies described in Northern tradition, the earliest of which was originated by Mahāvīra's own son-in-law, and arose in his lifetime. But the schism of 79 B.C. was a profound one, in no way comparable to the imperceptible impregnation of primitive Buddhism by the *Great Vehicle.* The Southern group consists of the Digambaras: as the name indicates, they are those who remain faithful to Mahāvīra by wearing no clothing, while the other branch, the Śvetāmbaras, resume, or perhaps never abandon, the white garment, more suited to the Northern climate. It is perhaps going a little too far to identify these Śvetāmbaras with the adherents of the old Pārśva sect, on the presumption that the movement had survived through the centuries.

The austerity of their habits matches their doctrine. In Europe (and in India too, I fear) little is known of the ancient Digambaras. We do know that they repudiated the Canon as we have it today, holding that after the death of Jina the old texts had disappeared stage by stage and had been replaced by new ones. They therefore set up a kind of substitute Canon, a collection of 'four Vedas', which they themselves, presumably, do not claim as authentic.

Let us now consider the very important question of the Jaina Canon. The first Council, that of Pāṭaliputra, was held under Bhadrabāhu, in the fourth century B.C. Like most Councils, its chief aim was to collect the texts into one body and to define the extent of the authentic scriptures. In this it resembled the Buddhist Councils, especially the second Council, at Vaiśālī, which also took place in the fourth century; its object, according to Southern tradition, was the establishment of the Canon, but it is far more probable that its real purpose was to combat the Mahāsāṃghika schism, just as the Jaina Council was really directed against the Digambaras.

However this may be, the Jaina Scriptures were beginning to fall into a corrupt state; it was already too late to save the twelfth and last of the *Aṅgas*, or basic texts, in its entirety. The Jainas, in fact, have a tradition that the Canon does not wholly derive from Mahāvīra's teaching. Part of it is thought to have been drawn up by Bhadrabāhu. As late as the fifth century A.D., the Council of Valabhī made a final compilation, their object being to establish the form of the texts after the secession of the Digambaras: the version adopted at Valabhī is the one we have today, a version established nine centuries after the Master's lifetime. But the composition of the collections themselves must date back much further; the tradition that the main work of elaborating the Canonical Scriptures took place in a short period of two centuries, between the death of Vīra and the time of Bhadrabāhu, may not be far from the truth. The fact that the Digambaras reject this tradition must not be allowed to prejudice the facts; and it will be the task of future scholars to pursue this problem by means of textual criticism of the Canon itself, according to the method so brilliantly demonstrated by Schubring.[1]

We cannot hope to know what the very earliest form of the Canon was. It may have been found in its entirety in those *pūrvas*, 'prior' or 'primordial' texts, which were lost after their substance had been incorporated into the twelfth *Aṅga*, a work that was also lost at a later date.

In spite of all these vicissitudes, it must be admitted that the Jaina Canon gives an impression of greater antiquity than the Buddhist Canon. The work as a whole, which is also called the *piṭaka* or 'basket', is arranged less systematically; it contains some independent texts; the interpolations are more easily recognizable as such. Its 'philosophical' portion and the Pāli *Abhidhamma* cover no common ground. Finally, there is only one single tradition, nothing of the diversity of the Buddhist schools. On the other hand, we note that the Jainas, being more concerned with technology than the Buddhists, have included treatises on cosmography, mathematics and other semi-secular matters, after the fashion of the Brahmanical *Vedāṅgas*.

Despite internal dissensions, the influence of the community seems to have spread fairly rapidly. The migration to the South, if it really took place, must have been the origin of a vast group that still exists today, but which is not so numerous as the Northern groups. The latter first spread to Orissâ (where the Canon seems to have attracted the interest of King Khāravela), and then to Bengal; and they early reached the North-West, where the extraordinarily rich finds at Mathurā are evidence that a community flourished there at a very ancient date.

The periods when Jainism enjoyed royal protection

[1] In nearly all his works, from the earliest, *Das Kalpasūtra* (Leipzig, 1905), down to the most recent, *Studien zum Mahānisīha*, by F.-R. Hamm and W. Schubring (Hamburg, 1951). Cf. also his comprehensive study, *Die Lehre der Jainas, nach den alten Quellen dargestellt* (Berlin and Leipzig, 1935).

were those of its greatest activity; when such favour was withdrawn, its influence was greatly restricted. This is true of Buddhism also. In the South, the most flourishing period was under the *Rāṣṭrakūṭas* in the ninth century; in the twelfth century a decline set in, and from then on we find evidence of persecutions, first under the Southern Gurjaras, and later under the Pāṇḍyas. As in the case of Buddhism, the influence of Rāmānuja and the Śrīvaiṣṇavas brought about wholesale conversions to Vaiṣṇavism. Under the Cōḷas came the more violent attack of the Vīraśaivas, who destroyed temples and archives and harrassed the commercial classes, the mainstay of the whole community. The Jainas have been more severely affected by economic vicissitudes than any other sect. Finally, we must bear in mind the effects of Moslem oppression, both in the North and in the South, though they were, of course, more pronounced in the North.

In the North, the Gujarāti country became the principal centre. A decline set in in other areas, especially in those Eastern regions where Jainism had originated. Indian religious movements tend to become established far from their original homeland, where they leave little trace. Moreover, some of the Gujarāti Kings were interested in Jaina art, as was Kumārapāla in the thirteenth century, for instance, the patron of the famous Hemacandra who set himself to transform the kingdom into a model Jaina state.

In the last analysis, the progress made balanced the setbacks, and the community has always been quite firmly established. It forms a strange contrast with Buddhism, which was far more spectacularly successful in its origins and which early enjoyed imperial support. I do not believe that one movement suffered more than the other from persecution; but it may be that Jainism adopted a more compliant attitude towards the civil power, and that its opposition to Hinduism was less pronounced. The chief cause, however, is to be sought elsewhere. It was the strength, and yet at the same time the weakness of Buddhism that it drew its adherents largely from among the poor, whereas Jainism turned to the rich and influential. Again, the monasteries are an essential part of Buddhist life; if the monasteries are destroyed, the blow is mortal. In Jainism, the lay community has a far greater relative importance; it plays its part in the administration of its religion and in the cult. Jainism is in fact just what it claims to be, a fourfold Church, a fourfold *tīrtha*, composed, that is to say, of monks, nuns, and male and female lay followers. Another advantage is the great richness of the extra-Canonical literature, which greatly surpasses that of the Buddhists, in its variety of *genre*, at any rate; these works, moreover, are to be found in all the local languages, Tamil, Kanarese, Gujarāti, to say nothing of Sanskrit and Middle Indian: all these factors contribute to the strength of the Jaina position.

Finally, the very stability of the doctrine may have contributed to its survival. It never underwent any process comparable to the general re-assessment of values attendant on the transition from the *Hīnayāna* to the *Mahāyāna*. As we have seen, it suffered a violent schism that resulted in a wide gulf separating two groups; and if we are inclined to think the cause trifling, we must remember that nothing is trifling where religious matters are concerned. But nevertheless, on both sides of the gulf the same doctrine, ethics and philosophy were retained, and this scission proved to be the only one.

Of course, as always happens everywhere in India, many sects arose; among the Northern Jainas there are said to be eighty-four sects, called *gacchas*. Tradition maintains that several of them go back to Pārśva. It is also said, more credibly, that they arose in the tenth century. Among the Digambaras, the divisions seem to have taken place earlier, but they are fewer in number: only four groups or *gaṇas* are found. Each group possesses genealogical tables of its own, recorded in special texts which are not infrequently confirmed by inscriptional evidence; like the Buddhists, and in contrast to the Hindus, the Jainas have a strong historical sense. But the sectarian divisions do not indicate the slightest doctrinal divergence. These Jaina groups are not so much sects in the Hindu sense (for these are often aggressively insistent in their philosophical claims) as brotherhoods, rather like our monastic communities.

The Sthānakvāsīs of the eighteenth century are not in quite the same position: they are indeed a reformed sect, who, rejecting image-worship and temple services, seek to return to the ancient form of Jainism. Movements advocating a return to the past, whether they make a lasting appeal or not, are recurrent in Hinduism; there is no need to invoke Islamic influence to explain the occurrence of such a slogan. But the Sthānakvāsīs go further, by also rejecting part of the Canon. Yet it is not certain that in India even this would be sufficient to constitute a heresy. Moreover, there had been a sixteenth-century precedent in an analogous movement, that of the Lumpākas, which seems to have come to nothing.

Reforming zeal constantly manifests itself; and founders of new sects quickly pass into oblivion in India. Four years ago, I paid a visit to the sect of the Terāpanthīs, who were holding their annual assembly in a country town in Rājputānā. This group, whose name means 'those who follow the path of the Thirteen', was founded in 1760 by a Sthānakvāsī layman called Bhikanji. Bhikanji was motivated by the conviction that his co-religionists had fallen away from the primitive customs of the movement. He wanted to return to these early ways, and founded a group of which he became the first pontiff; the present pontiff is the ninth of the line. To be present at a gathering of the Terāpanthīs is to have experience of the life of a sect which makes every effort to return to the precepts and customs of the time of Mahāvīra. The scene is pleasantly picturesque, with its rustic setting, and its central dais decorated with banners of naïve design; in the assembly the monks and nuns are carefully segregated from each other, and from the crowds who have come out of curiosity, though they too are attentive and devout in appearance. The alternating chant of the religious, with the crowd taking up the refrain in chorus, provides an interlude in the sermon, preached in the Master's vibrant tones; as he preaches, his face has the fervency of an apostle; he is like a Mahāvīra *redivivus*. The rule of the Terāpanthīs is extremely severe; for these wandering ascetics must renounce almost everything and beg their scanty food all their lives. It is not unusual to see one of them (as I have) freely choose to die in the way characteristic of the Jainas, ending a life of austerities by abstaining from food altogether. Nevertheless, it is a way of life that many aspire after eagerly; postulants beseech the Master to admit them to it; relations and friends add their entreaties on the applicant's behalf. Such is religious fanaticism in India, where the secular life is accounted of little value in comparison with the rewards won by following the path of mysticism.

In order to trace in detail the history of the Jaina Church it would first be necessary to make a critical examination of the enormous mass of literature, partly narrative, partly moral in intention, that the Jainas, the most prolix of the Hindus, have poured out in the course of centuries. In some cases they have falsified historical fact in their eagerness to convert princes and high dignitaries; thus, they allege that Candragupta Maurya became a Jaina and ended his life as an ascetic in Mysore, among the community that had migrated there. Some sources claim as patrons of Jainism the Emperor Aśoka, the legendary Vikramāditya, the Hephtalite king Toramāṇa, and many more.

We have already mentioned the conservative tendencies of Jaina thought. It is true that the later literature carries us a long way from the sources in the luxuriant imagination it displays. The developments in iconography, the establishment of the great shrines and the public worship that grew up with them, all these factors seemed to combine to deflect mediaeval Jainism into new paths; but despite all this, its great moral and philosophical principles have remained stable, and religious feeling has probably not altered greatly. If we turn to Hinduism for a parallel, we have only to ask ourselves how much real effect the frenzied Śivas and grimacing Kālīs of common representation produced on Śaṅkara and the brotherhood he founded.

The fact that there are Brahman priests or *pūjārīs* employed in the service of the Jaina temples emphasizes the lack of a secular clergy in religions of a monastic type like Buddhism and Jainism. Any features taken over from Hinduism have taken on a Jainist aspect; one has only to consider the way in which Indian heroes are treated in Jaina legend. Tantrism, which corrupted other systems of thought, Buddhism included, produced only a limited effect on Jainism, manifested by the sudden appearance of many female divinities, long-delayed descendants of Kālī and Tārā.

The monastic rule was the Jainas' greatest creation. It is a severe rule, dominated by the conception of non-violence, *ahiṃsā*, a conception which the Jainas may perhaps have originated, in their attitude of reaction against Vedic 'violence'. The monks and nuns are called *bhikṣu* and *bhikṣuṇī*, as in Buddhism. The five monastic vows, designed for the attainment of ataraxy, are negative ones, as are the five *yamas* or abstentions of *Yoga*, with which they are identical: not to do violence, not to lie, not to steal, not to have sexual intercourse, not to have possessions. The first four correspond to the *sīlas* or the *śikṣāpadas* of Buddhism, which are usually expressed in expanded form in ten precepts. But their real provenance is probably an ancient code which both the Brahmanical *saṃnyāsins* and the *bhikṣus* drew upon. Jaina asceticism grew up out of a background of pan-Indian, or perhaps pre-Indian, asceticism, which can be traced also in Buddhism, though Buddhism early repudiated it. What are the *dhutāṅgas*, those practices of the Pāli Canon appropriate to the *dhuta* (called the *avadhūta* in Brahmanical asceticism) but survivals of an ancient code of asceticism which must have been abolished or suppressed in common usage? Primitive Buddhism was probably closer to Jainism than the form revealed in the Canon. Not only did it lay more emphasis on asceticism, but it must have prescribed that regular alternation between the wandering and the sedentary life that preceded the institution of permanent *vihāras*; this alternation is clearly recognized in the Jaina Canon, but the Pāli Canon regards it as a practice borrowed from what it calls the *titthiyas* or heretics. This system, again, was probably modelled on the cycle that governs the life of the *brahmacārin*, who enters once more upon a period of study when the rainy season sets in.

The precept of non-violence manifests itself in forms that remained peculiar to Jainism, and which may perhaps appear somewhat naïve in our eyes—the broom made of white wool with which the devout sweep clear the path they are about to tread, and the mask placed in front of the mouth so that no living matter shall be breathed in.

The Jaina rule is characterized by severe and exacting prescriptions. The day is divided into four periods, and the way in which the time is spent is strictly regulated. Rules are laid down for every detail, even to the amount of food that the monk may take daily (thirty-two mouthfuls of the size of an egg), and the conditions under which he may accept lodging for the night, for he must take his food in a different place from that in which he spends the night. The practice of austerities is carried to great lengths: physical asceticism is practised by keeping the body in unnatural positions, and especially by fasting: total fasting for relatively short periods and partial fasting, which assumes various forms, and may last for as long as 522 days. More importance was probably attached to fasting in the primitive form of Buddhism; but the *uposatha* (the term that describes it, and which is itself a borrowed word) is really only a day of abstention from work and an official festival, like the Vedic *upavasatha* that took place on the eve of some of the great ceremonies.

Mental asceticism consists of progressive exercises in concentration, by which a higher state of consciousness, that of *kevalin*, may be attained in fourteen modes. The same word *kevalin* is used to denote Liberation according to the *Sāṃkhya*, and the technique bears an obvious relationship to *Yoga*. The fourteen modes, strangely enough, are not successive stages following one another in time; they are like a keyboard over which the spirit ranges, moving up or down as the nature of its actions fluctuates. An extreme form of asceticism takes the form of committing suicide by abstaining from food. This is called *saṃlekhanā*, a term that suggests the idea of self-inflicted suffering, and which, according to the texts, properly denotes the receding of the sensible world and of sensation that is the preliminary to a death-fast. The term is known in Buddhist tradition, in which it designates certain severe macerations. It is also to be compared with the *saṃlikhitam* of the *Atharvaveda*, which is applied to the ruined gambler, a man who has been 'completely cleaned out', as we say in familiar speech. One's impression is that suicide by fasting, which is certainly not unknown in Buddhist tradition and in Hinduism in general as far back as Vedic times, has been promoted by the Jainas to the status of a religious institution; the inauguration of the fast is regarded as a sacrament, and is accompanied by a re-affirmation of vows, solemn renunciation, and so on.

Another characteristic practice is that of public confession. This is a feature that Jainism shares with Buddhism, and the Jaina term *pratikramaṇa*, which means 'return', 'way back', is not far removed from the Pāli term *pāṭidesanīya*, denoting the sins to be confessed, or literally 'to be related by turning back'. In Jainism, confession of a sin committed at night takes place in the morning, and that of a sin committed during the day, in the evening; a more solemn confession takes place at the end of a fortnight, as with the Buddhists. The man making the confession acknowledges his faults, becomes spiritually purified, and expresses his desire for improvement. It seems likely that in the mechanical way in which it functions, and in the power of completely wiping out *karman* that is inherent in it, the Jaina confession represents an earlier evaluation than the more refined Buddhist conception, in which repentance plays an important part. This distinction is in accordance with the general opposition between the automatism, or perhaps it might be called the realism of the Jainas, and the Buddhist preoccupation with ethical values, which represents a further stage of reflection. The last day of the period of wandering life is marked by a general confession, which thus terminates the active part of the religious life and also coincides with the end of the Jaina year; this confession is the counterpart of the Buddhist confession that marks the end of the rainy season, and constitutes a feature of what is known as the *pravāraṇā* or 'closing'.

Ten degrees of expiation are prescribed in Jainism; firstly, there are corporal punishments, which resemble the voluntary practices of asceticism; then comes a 'cutting down' of the monk's seniority, which entails beginning again from the 'root', i.e. from the initiation; and lastly, expulsion from the community. *Parihāra* is a kind of segregation of a monk who is being punished or arraigned, and is comparable to the Buddhist *parivāsa*, which is a probationary period of supervision. Transgression is known by the Vedāntic term *māyā*, a veil obscuring true knowledge.

So much for the monks. As for the laymen, it is amazing to see how detailed and rigorous were the rules laid down for them in ancient times. Confession is in principle obligatory for them, and they are allowed to undertake the death-fast. They have twelve vows to observe, whereas the monks have only five; this is no doubt because secular life is more varied than monastic life. They too have a mystical scale, comprising eleven stages (*pratimā*), by which they can attain to a state as meritorious as that of the monks, and which is perhaps more difficult of attainment by reason of the worldly temptations that beset them; on reaching the eleventh stage, the layman is, in fact, a monk. Here there is a noticeable contrast between the Jaina and the Buddhist viewpoints, for Buddhism, at any rate in Pāli tradition, devotes relatively little attention to the *upāsakas*. But admittedly, it is on this point that the Jaina attitude has most relaxed its severity between early times and the present day.

Other aspects of this religion are no less highly developed. Its cosmography, for example, is founded on the same principles as that of Buddhism and Brahmanism, but the terminology has been revised. The world, seen in cross-section horizontally, has as its axis a disc, a conception deriving from the Cosmic Support of the *Atharvaveda*. At the centre of the disc stands Mount Meru; around Meru lies Jambudvīpa, the island of the rose-apple tree; six mountains lie across it, and a sea encompasses it. The other continents are also envisaged as concentric islands, indefinite in number, each one encircled by a sea; a vast ocean embraces the whole. In the Buddhist conception, the four principal islands surrounding Meru are situated at the four cardinal points. This is an ancient scheme found also in the *Mahābhārata*. Concentric islands and seas are unknown to the *Mahābhārata*, though the idea is adopted in later Hinduism, and they are established as seven in number. The Jaina conception appears less archaic in this matter than in others.

As a vertical cross-section of the world, instead of the cosmic Egg of other systems, the Jainas envisage a complex figure, in the form of a triple pyramid or of a figure of eight. In the post-Canonical texts, this portrayal evolves into a human figure, the *Lokapuruṣa*, a reminiscence of the Vedic *Puruṣa*. The successive series of heavens form the head and the breast; the earth is represented by the waist, where the figure narrows; the lower half of the body represents the layers of subterranean worlds. The different spheres are each inhabited by beings appropriate to them, from the great gods and the *siddhas* or 'perfect' beings, down to the demons. This construction is linked with a mythology in which, side by side with the lesser gods, whose power is limited, and who arise from *karman* and are dependent upon it, we recognize more powerful gods, Śakra, Īśāna, Sanatkumāra, who are barely recognizable representatives of the Brahmanical gods Indra, Śiva and Brahman. One curious feature is the division of the divine beings into castes; the Trāyastriṃśas, for example, are administrators in high authority; the Lokapālas are guardians of order, and so on.

The representations of the infernal regions are among the most elaborate ever devised by the Indians. The seven hells are a reflection of the seven *pātālas* of the Brahmans; as in the Brahmanical conception, both the tormentors and the tormented are human beings, and there are no demons; torture by cold, a conception characteristic of Buddhism, is unknown, at least in ancient Jainism.

Finally, it should be noticed that the conception of a Supreme Being, to which Hinduism attained by such slow and painful stages, is just as foreign to Jainism as it probably was to Buddhism.

As a parallel to their cosmology, the Jainas' conception of time is one of indefinite extension, and this, as we know, is quite opposed to Vedic representations. Like post-Vedic Brahmanism, Jainism asserts that humanity has experienced a progressive decline, the *avasarpiṇī*. The bad era in which we are living, the fifth, began soon after the death of Mahāvīra (and therefore well after the beginning of the *kali* age of Hinduism). It will be followed by an even worse era before humanity enters upon the *utsarpiṇī*, the period of ascent. These six ages are obviously an expanded form of the four ages so frequently described in other systems; the pendulum-like course through decline to ascent is reminiscent of the day and night of Brahman.

All Indian sects have their speculative side; they consider problems relating to what we should call metaphysics, and develop literatures of varying extent on the subject. Although this aspect of the thought of a sect cannot really be separated from its general religious practices, it will be expedient to give a very brief account of the subject here.

In the first place, Jainism is an *ātmavāda*; it recognizes the Self or *jīva* as a stable, immaterial and eternal principle, endowed with consciousness and initiating action. This doctrine is, of course, diametrically opposed to that of Buddhism, but it is in accordance with the spirit of the *Upaniṣads* and the *Vedānta*.

The theory of *karman*, the keystone of the system, is conceived in principle much as it is in other systems, but, in conformity with the general trend of Jaina thought, it takes on a classificatory and encyclopaedic character. *Karman* is a real substance, a sort of poison that infects the soul and renders it liable to be invaded by the other substances, space and time. The procedure is to destroy former *karman* and ward off the approach of new *karman*; this is accomplished by asceticism and the other methods of purification, both ritual and mental. *Karman* not only determines the destiny of the soul; it imparts a permanent quality to it, called *leśyā*, a word as yet unexplained. *Leśyā* is a kind of reflection cast on the soul by matter. Six kinds are recognized, each one having its own particular colour (and this is the most important distinction), its own texture perceptible to the touch, its own taste and duration; they correspond to the ethical state of the creature in relation to his own plane, whether it be human, divine, demoniac or animal.

As in current Hindu teaching, *saṃsāra*, the indefinitely prolonged transmigration of souls, is linked with the theory of *karman*. Thus the Jainas have taken over *en masse* the conceptions that were dimly perceptible amid the confusion of Indian thought of the post-Vedic period, *ātman*, *karman*, *saṃsāra*. The state of liberation is conceived of as being enjoyed in the highest part of heaven, a mountain-peak. There the *siddha*, or liberated one, dwells, freed from the body, yet occupying a position in space, a two-dimensional being, in fact. He possesses full consciousness and infinite power, but he makes no use of it (a conception of supererogatory endowment that is typically Indian), for his state is one of absolute repose. This conception is, if I am not mistaken, close to that of *nirvāṇa* according to *Hīnayāna* or *Sāṃkhya*. In later representations, either activist conceptions are introduced, or else there appears the idea of the *unio mystica*, which profoundly modified not only the nature of Liberation, but also the means by which it is attained.

I think these observations have sufficed to show that the Jaina movement presents evidence that is of great interest, both for the historical and comparative study of religion in ancient India and for the history of religion in general. Based on profoundly Indian elements, it is at the same time a highly original creation, containing very ancient material, more ancient than that of Buddhism, and yet more highly refined and elaborated.

Few religions have made less effort to spread their doctrines. Jainism has never been in any way a missionary religion, as Buddhism has always been and as Hinduism itself has been from time to time. The archaeological evidences of Jainism discovered in one region of Central Asia are a purely chance phenomenon.

At the present day, certain Jaina groups are at last spreading propaganda outside their own territory, by issuing pamphlets and establishing centres. The time is certainly opportune for them to expound the merits of their fundamental guiding principle, that of non-violence. Only the future can decide whether an attempt of this nature has any hope of success. Jainism does not lack influential and devoted lay-followers, who would be ready to give their patronage and support, nor is there any dearth of scholars interested in its origins and literary tradition; there are in fact today proportionally more scholars working in this field than in any other branch of Indian studies. But its contemporary thinkers have not succeeded in advancing beyond the domain of commentary; as for the ascetics, their knowledge is by definition incommunicable, if not undemonstrable. The chief need of the Jainas is, in fact, for great spiritual leaders, leaders such as Hinduism has produced more than once, even in recent times.

INDEX

i. General

ii. Bibliographical